Section Four — Writing Techniques

Section Five — Exam Techniques

Section Six — The Exam

Section Seven — Sample Answers

Published by CGP

Editors:
Joe Brazier
Charley Darbishire
Rachael Powers
Katherine Reed
Edward Robinson
Caley Simpson

Produced With:
Alison Smith
Peter Thomas
Nicola Woodfin

Contributors:
Caroline Bagshaw
Lorraine Campbell
Graham Fletcher
Jane Harrison
Terry Hyde
Nicola Woodfin

ISBN: 978 1 84146 878 5

With thanks to Heather Gregson, John Sanders and Jeffrey Emmett for the proofreading.
With thanks to Laura Stoney for the copyright research.

The Publisher would like to thank the following copyright holders for permission to reproduce texts and images:

With thanks to iStockphoto.com for permission to reproduce the photograph used on page 43.

With thanks to Octagon-uk.com for permission to use the article on page 44.

Page 44: Photograph © Sipa Press / Rex Features

With thanks to Habitat for Humanity for permission to use the webpage on page 45.

Every effort has been made to locate copyright holders and obtain permission to reproduce texts and images. For those texts and images where it has been difficult to trace the originator of the work, we would be grateful for information. If any copyright holder would like us to make an amendment to the acknowledgements, please notify us and we will gladly update the book at the next reprint. Thank you.

Groovy website: www.cgpbooks.co.uk
Jolly bits of clipart from CorelDRAW®
Printed by Elanders Ltd, Newcastle upon Tyne.

Based on the classic CGP style created by Richard Parsons.

How to Use This Book

This book will help you do better in <u>Section A</u> of your <u>Unit 1 exam</u> for <u>GCSE English</u> or <u>GCSE English Language</u>. This part of the exam is on "Understanding non-fiction texts", which can mean newspaper and magazine articles, travel writing, adverts, biographies — basically anything that's not made up.

You need to show these Skills in the Exam

To do well in this part of the exam, you need to be able to do these <u>important things</u>:

1) <u>Understand</u> what a text is <u>telling you</u> and use good <u>examples</u> from the text to back up your points. You'll also have to <u>compare</u> texts (say how they're similar and how they're different) and use <u>examples</u> to back up your points.

2) Explain how writers use <u>language</u>, <u>grammar</u>, <u>layout</u> and <u>structure</u> to make their writing <u>effective</u>. You'll also have to say <u>how effective</u> you think a text is at getting its <u>message</u> across to the <u>reader</u>.

'Text' just means a piece of writing.

The 'reader' is just anyone who's reading the text.

The book's Organised Like This

SECTION 1 discusses the <u>audience</u> (who the author is writing for) and the <u>purpose</u> (why they're writing). There are examples of different kinds of <u>non-fiction texts</u> and how to write about them.

SECTION 2 has plenty of tips on how to <u>follow an argument</u> and how to write about one. It explains the techniques that writers use to <u>argue a point</u>, and how they work.

SECTION 3 is about the <u>presentation</u> and <u>layout</u> of texts — how the way they <u>look</u> affects how they come across to the reader.

SECTION 4 is all about <u>writing techniques</u> — how writers use <u>language</u> and <u>structure</u> to make their work more effective.

SECTION 5 gives you loads of <u>tips</u> on what you can do in the <u>exam</u> to get <u>great marks</u>.

SECTION 6 contains a <u>mock exam</u>, so you know what the real thing will look like.

SECTION 7 shows you the <u>mark scheme</u> for the mock exam in Section 6. Then there are loads of <u>sample answers</u>, working up from an <u>E grade</u> to a <u>C grade</u>.

At the end of the book there's a handy <u>glossary</u> that gives you <u>definitions</u> of loads of important <u>words and terms</u> that you might need.

The book also doubles up as a rather fetching hat...

This book is full of straightforward ways of getting <u>extra marks</u>. Read through the notes and examples. Practise all the tips. Then try to use what you've learnt in your work.

The Audience

When you're reading a non-fiction text, you've got to think about the <u>audience</u> — the people the writer wants to read their work.

The Audience is the People who read the text

The writer will always have a <u>certain group of people</u> in mind as their audience when they write.

e.g.

TEXT	AUDIENCE
Article in 'The Financial Times'	Business people
Travel guide book	Holiday-makers
Problem page in 'Sugar'	Teenage girls

Content and Presentation can show who the Audience is

1) Sometimes you can work out who the audience is by the text's <u>content</u> (subject matter), e.g. an article in 'Top Gear' magazine about cars is obviously aimed at someone who's into cars.

2) The <u>presentation</u> can also tell you who the target audience is. E.g. a book with a <u>large, simple font</u> and lots of <u>pictures</u> is probably for children.

The font is the style of lettering used. There are formal fonts and informal fonts.

Language can give you plenty of clues too

1) The <u>vocabulary</u> (choice of words) can tell you about the target audience, e.g. about the <u>age group</u>:

> Today, we witnessed a discussion on foxhunting. This issue elicited mixed emotions.

Difficult vocabulary, e.g. saying 'elicited' instead of just 'brought out', shows this text is aimed at adults.

> Dungeon Killer 3 is the hottest new game of the year! There are 52 amazing levels.

Modern slang, e.g. 'hottest new game' shows this is aimed at younger people.

2) The language can also give you clues about the target audience's <u>level of understanding</u>:

> The object of a game of football is to get the ball in the opposing team's goal. It might sound easy, but it's a very skilful game.

Simple explanations show this is for beginners.

> The next hole was a par-3 and I hit my tee shot directly onto the green. Sadly my putting let me down badly and I ended up getting a bogey.

Technical words show this is for people who know a bit about the sport.

Hello? Is there anybody there?

You need to work out who the target audience is. For example, is the writer aiming their work at children? Or are they aiming it at adults? It'll have a big impact on the way the text is written.

The Purpose of the Text

Another big thing you need to work out about the texts you get in the exam is: "What is the writer's <u>purpose</u>?" In other words, "<u>Why</u> has the writer written this?" Why indeed.

There are four Common Purposes of writing

The <u>purpose</u> of the text means the <u>reason</u> that it has been written — what the writer is <u>trying to do</u>. Non-fiction texts are usually written for <u>one or more</u> of these reasons:

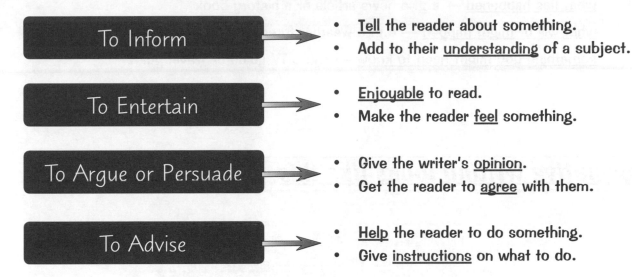

To Inform
- <u>Tell</u> the reader about something.
- Add to their <u>understanding</u> of a subject.

To Entertain
- <u>Enjoyable</u> to read.
- Make the reader <u>feel</u> something.

To Argue or Persuade
- Give the writer's <u>opinion</u>.
- Get the reader to <u>agree</u> with them.

To Advise
- <u>Help</u> the reader to do something.
- Give <u>instructions</u> on what to do.

Pages 4-7 tell you how to spot which of these purposes the writer has in mind, and how you can <u>discuss</u> them in the exam.

You also need to know about Tone and Style

1) The different <u>tones</u> that writers can use are like the different <u>tones of voice</u> when people speak, e.g. calm, angry, friendly — see pages 10-11.

2) <u>Style</u> is to do with the type of language and techniques a writer uses, for example formal or informal — see pages 8-9.

3) Writers choose a style and tone that suits the <u>audience</u> they're writing for and the <u>purpose</u> of their writing.

> When you're reading a non-fiction text, remember to think about:
> - <u>who</u> the author is writing for (audience)
> - what they're <u>trying to do</u> (purpose)
> - <u>how</u> they write (style and tone)
> - how much you think they <u>succeed</u>.

WARNING: Being too informal can lead to dire consequences.

My life has no purpose — but I do have a dog that barks...

Some texts have more than one purpose, e.g. travel books are generally meant to entertain, as they're full of interesting little stories, but they're usually informative too, as they tell you great places to go where you won't meet other tourists — unless they've read the book as well, that is.

Informative Texts

Some texts have the purpose of <u>informing</u>. This means the writer's aim is to pass on knowledge to you as clearly as possible. Informative texts have lots of <u>facts</u> and usually a <u>straightforward style</u>.

Informative Writing Tells You something

Informative texts give the reader <u>facts and information</u>. This could be:

- <u>what has happened</u> — e.g. a news article or a history book
- <u>what will or might happen</u> — e.g. a weather forecast
- <u>something you might need to know</u> — e.g. a **TV guide** or travel guide

Informative Writing looks like this

Gives you specific details and dates.

The Mini first went on sale in 1959. It soon became the best selling car in Europe. Over five million of them were made and many famous people including The Beatles bought them.

The Mini Cooper S version won the Monte Carlo Rally in 1964.

Contains facts rather than opinions.

Write about informative texts Like This

Make a clear opening point.

Use quotes to back up your points.

Build on your ideas.

The author gives a positive impression of the Mini by giving a lot of details about its history. The fact that "Over five million of them were made" proves that they were very popular. This is added to when the author tells us that "famous people including the Beatles bought them". This fact shows that the cars were successful and fashionable.

Explain the effect of the quote.

If there are lots of facts and figures, it's informative...

You need to show you can recognise informative writing and explain how it's used. Think about what the writer is informing us about, why they're doing it and how effective you think they are.

Entertaining Texts

Entertaining writing is stuff that you would read for <u>pleasure</u>. It has lots of the kind of things that make you <u>scared</u>, <u>excited</u> or <u>amused</u>. That's more of the fun stuff, then...

Entertaining Writing aims to be Enjoyable to read

1) Entertaining writing is meant to be <u>interesting</u>. People read it for <u>fun</u>.
   Travel books are a good example of entertaining non-fiction writing.

2) The author might entertain the reader with stories of <u>funny things</u> that happened to them.
   Or they might use <u>entertaining descriptions</u> of things or people.

3) Entertaining writing has more <u>creative</u> and <u>unexpected</u> bits than informative writing.

Entertaining Writing looks like this

This piece of writing is on the same subject as the one on page 4 — but this one is <u>entertaining</u>. Have a look at how it's different from the informative one.

> My first car was a 1970 Mini. I loved it from the moment I sat in it. It went like a rocket. By that I mean it always had smoke coming out of its rear end! Perhaps I shouldn't have tried to drive it like Michael Caine.
>
> It was a subtle shade of bright orange and should have come complete with free executive sunglasses. Still, I was a student then and they wouldn't have fitted my image.

Interesting comparisons.

Contains funny images.

Tells a story about real life.

Write about entertaining texts Like This

Make an opening point.

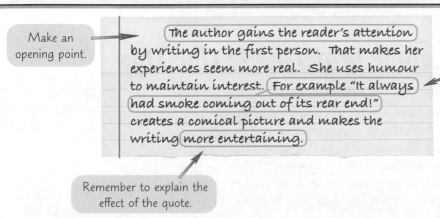

The author gains the reader's attention by writing in the first person. That makes her experiences seem more real. She uses humour to maintain interest. For example "It always had smoke coming out of its rear end!" creates a comical picture and makes the writing more entertaining.

Use evidence from the text.

Remember to explain the effect of the quote.

Nobby found the new Bill Bryson book most entertaining.

Writing exam answers — now that's entertainment...

Some texts will be both informative and entertaining, e.g. a travel book may contain useful facts about a place but also give you some funny stories about what happened when the author was there. Try to work out which bits of the text inform and which entertain when you write about them.

Texts that Argue or Persuade

One purpose of writing is to <u>argue</u> a point, to try to get the reader to agree with it. Some texts go a stage further and try to <u>persuade</u> you to actually do something.

Arguing and Persuading are similar

1) When people write to <u>argue</u>, they want to make the reader <u>agree with their opinion</u>. They try to write <u>clearly</u> and <u>forcefully</u> to make their opinions as strong as possible.

2) Sometimes writers try to <u>persuade</u> you to do something, e.g. support a political party or buy a new brand of washing powder. Persuasive writing often tries to <u>appeal to the reader</u> by using a <u>personal tone</u>.

Writing to Argue looks like this

Opinions clear from the start.

People who claim that young people are lazy are badly informed. The vast majority are anything but lazy. In a recent survey of 14-16 year olds, 76% said they had a Saturday job and another 6% did weekday paper rounds. Does that sound like laziness to you?

Statistics used to back up argument.

Question challenges the reader to think about the issue.

Persuasive writing looks like this

Clearly states what it wants the reader to do.

Are you fed up of being treated as second-rate by employers because you're under 18? By signing our petition you will help to send a message to the government that people under 18 are just as hard-working as everyone else.

Talks to the reader directly.

Write about texts that argue or persuade Like This

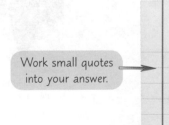
Work small quotes into your answer.

The writer argues his point very forcefully. He uses statistics to show that many young people have jobs and accuses those who disagree with him of being "badly informed". This suggests that anyone who thinks young people are lazy has not really thought the issue through.

Show how the writer's argument works.

Persuasive texts are great, don't you agree? Yes you do...

If a writer is trying to argue or persuade, it's all about getting the reader to see things from their point of view. The writer will give lots of evidence that supports their point of view.

Texts that Advise

When people write to advise, they're trying to help the reader to <u>do something</u>, or to make the right <u>decision</u>. The style is more straightforward and less emotional than writing that argues or persuades.

Writing to Advise sounds Clear and Calm

1) When people are writing to advise, they want their readers to <u>follow their suggestions</u>.

2) The tone will be <u>calm</u> and <u>less emotional</u> than writing that argues or persuades.

3) The advice will usually be <u>clearly written and laid out</u>. The writer may use bullet points or numbered lists to make it easier to follow.

4) There are lots of different types of texts which advise — ranging from <u>magazine problem pages</u> to <u>health advice leaflets</u>.

"Congratulations on purchasing your new TS-522/A shell..."

Writing to Advise looks like this

Talks to the reader by using "you".

Before you buy a pension, you need to be sure that it is the right one for you. You should look at the pension company's reputation, past results and penalties for changing schemes.

Uses details to give useful advice.

Write about texts that advise Like This

Use P.E.E. in your answers — Point, Example, Explanation. See page 35.

This is your point...

The writer uses a friendly, no-nonsense tone to get her advice across clearly. When she says, "you need to be sure", it sounds as if she is talking to a friend. This makes the reader more likely to take the advice.

The details of the advice, such as "look at the pension company's reputation", make the writer seem to know a lot about the subject. As a result of this, the reader is more likely to think that the advice is worthwhile.

... here's your example...

... and this bit explains the effect of language on the reader.

Texts that advise are clearly presented and easy to follow

Texts that advise usually assume you're already on the writer's side — people usually choose to read them because they want to know about something and they trust the writer's opinion. Because of this, they usually sound more friendly and less "in-your-face" than texts that argue or persuade.

Formal Style

Formal writing is writing that sounds polite or "correct" — the sort of writing you use in schoolwork. Informal writing is the opposite — a relaxed casual style, like the way you'd write to your mates.

There are a few ways of Spotting Formal Writing

1) Here are a few common features of formal writing:

- a dry or "stuffy" tone (not exciting or emotional)
- standard English — no slang or abbreviations
- long sentences with correct punctuation
- sounds impersonal — the writer doesn't try to relate to you

When the writer mentioned 'pâté' for the third time, Jeremy felt it related to him just a little too much.

2) Pieces of writing that are usually written in a formal style include:

- textbooks
- safety leaflets
- job adverts
- business letters
- instruction manuals
- news reports

3) Formal writing often has a stern, serious tone. It won't contain jokes or light-hearted comments.

Formal Writing looks like this

Long sentence.

Avoids shortened words — "it is" instead of "it's".

> When wiring an electrical plug it is always necessary to follow the safety instructions in order to avoid personal injury or death. It is easy to suffer serious harm and is simply not worth the risk. Some people believe that it is better to leave this kind of work to qualified electricians.

Sounds strict.

Opinion is given in an impersonal way — "Some people believe" instead of "I believe".

Write about formal writing Like This

Say what style the writer uses.

Give an example.

> The writer creates a formal style by using long sentences and avoiding talking directly to the reader. For example, he says "it is always necessary to" instead of "you have to". The formal style makes it clear that the information is important. I think it is effective because it gives an impression of how dangerous it would be if you did not follow the advice.

Say if you think it works and why.

One is undoubtedly required to discuss formal writing...

Basically, if a text sounds like it's been written by a teacher or a bank manager, it's formal. As usual, you need to say why the writer has chosen to use this style — think about who they're writing for and what message they're trying to give, and say how the formal style helps them do this.

Informal Style

Informal writing sounds as if someone is <u>chatting</u> to you. It sounds more <u>friendly</u> and <u>casual</u> than formal writing. Writers often use an informal style to try to build up a <u>relationship</u> with the reader.

Informal Writing sounds chatty

1) If writing is clearly <u>not formal</u>, it's — wait for it — <u>informal</u>. Tricky eh?

2) Here are a few common <u>features</u> of informal writing:

* chatty comments, as if the writer is talking to you
* non-standard English — e.g. abbreviations and slang
* short, simple sentences
* jokes and a light-hearted tone

Light-hearted Tone was a perfect match for Carefree Meg.

3) Pieces of writing that are often written in an <u>informal style</u> include:

* teenage magazine articles
* adverts aimed at young people
* gossip columns
* travel writing

Informal Writing looks like this

Friendly tone.

Contractions — "you'll", "don't".

> So, you want to wire a plug? Well, if you take my advice you'll find out how. Being a bright spark is one thing but you don't want to end up that way permanently, do you? You're probably better off letting somebody who knows their way around electrics do it for you.

Light-hearted comments.

Uses "you" and "my" — sounds personal.

Write about informal writing Like This

Informal slang phrases such as "bright spark" give the impression that the writer is just an ordinary person. By using humour like "you don't want to end up that way permanently, do you?", the writer makes an important point without seeming too serious.

Use an example for every point.

Explain how the language makes it sound informal.

Informal writing helps the reader relate to the writer...

The formality or informality of a piece of writing is all about the way it's expressed, rather than what it actually says. Remember to explain who the writing is aimed at, what the writer is trying to do, how the writer is trying to do it, and how well you think the writer has done it.

Personal Tone

The differences between personal and impersonal writing are again all to do with the style of writing. Personal writing sounds like the author is talking to you, while impersonal writing, er... doesn't.

Personal Writing sounds like it's talking to you

1) Personal writing is written in the first person — it uses "I", "me", "my" etc.
2) The writing is all from the writer's point of view. It's as if the author is talking to you.
3) Because it's from the writer's point of view, it's often biased. This means it expresses the author's personal opinions, rather than being neutral.
4) Personal writing often shows the author's emotions too, e.g. fear, happiness, anger.

Personal Writing looks like this

Personal opinion.

Written in first person.

School uniform should be banned. As if it isn't bad enough wearing a manky, itchy jumper most of the time, the PE kit we have to wear was designed for the 1950s. Mine was bought in Year 7 and it's ridiculously tight now. Then in Science, the lab coat and safety goggles make me look like a short-sighted lollipop lady.

Cheer up — you could look like this lot.

Write about personal writing Like This

Say what effect the personal tone has.

The personal tone allows the writer to express her views very directly. By writing in the first person, she seems to be speaking directly to the reader. She says her science clothes make her "look like a short-sighted lollipop lady". This humorous image shows how silly the uniform is and highlights the writer's feelings of embarrassment.

Work short quotes into your sentences.

Explain why the quote is effective.

Now it's personal...

Using a personal style allows the writer to tell you exactly how they feel, so it's good for expressing their emotions and opinions. On the down-side, the reader might not believe the writer as much as normal — the reader knows that it's just one person's opinion, and not necessarily a balanced view.

Impersonal Tone

With impersonal writing, the writer is <u>separate</u> from what they're writing about. There's no "I" or "we" — you're just told "this is what's going on", and it's presented as fact rather than opinion.

Impersonal Writing sounds Neutral and Detached

1) Impersonal writing is written in the <u>third person</u> — it uses "she", "him", "they" etc.

2) You don't get a sense of the writer's personality — it's as if it's written by an observer who is completely <u>separate</u> from what's happening.

3) Impersonal writing sounds <u>unemotional</u> and <u>factual</u>. There's usually a <u>neutral tone</u> — the writer doesn't seem to be taking sides.

4) Some <u>opinions</u> might be included — but written in such a serious, formal way that they <u>sound like they could be facts</u> (see bias on page 17).

Impersonal Writing looks like this

Sounds unemotional and factual.

Uniforms are often expensive — especially if schools require them to be bought from specific retailers. 80% of young people would prefer to wear their own clothes to school. Jonathan Langley, a head teacher in Gosforth, says that, "It's only a matter of time before school uniforms are phased out".

Neutral tone — the writer's opinion is never stated openly.

Write about impersonal writing Like This

The writer uses an impersonal tone to describe the drawbacks of school uniforms. Comments like "Uniforms are often expensive" and "80% of young people would prefer to wear their own clothes" sound factual and neutral. This helps persuade the reader that school uniforms are unpopular and unfair.

Make a clear opening point.

Comment on the use of language.

Use the P.E.E. method — see page 35.

Work out what impression the writer tries to give...

Watch out for writers who at first seem to be neutral. Even if they don't say "this is my opinion", they can still try to give a particular impression of something. Impersonal writing can be just as opinionated as personal writing — it's just a different way of presenting the writer's ideas.

Features of an Argument

If you're going to talk about a writer's argument in your answer, the first thing you need to do is <u>follow</u> the argument — in other words, <u>understand what points they're making</u>.

Look out for the Main Features of an Argument

A writer can use lots of different <u>techniques</u> when they argue a point. They could include:

- <u>facts</u> which back up their argument.
- <u>opinions</u> — either the author's or someone else's.
- <u>implications</u> — where the writer suggests something is the case without saying it outright, e.g. "Ever since Kevin moved in, things have started mysteriously disappearing."
- <u>rhetoric</u> and <u>bias</u> — see pages 16-17.

You have to be able to spot <u>when</u> one of these features turns up in the text, and say what <u>effect</u> it has.

Identify the Key Points of the argument

To follow an argument, you need to work out what the <u>key points</u> are — the main reasons the writer gives to back up their argument.

You can often spot where each new key point begins by the writer's use of paragraphs. A <u>new paragraph</u> often means a <u>new key point</u>:

> In this increasingly stressful age it is important that young people find the time to relax and enjoy the best years of their life. With exam after exam, modern teenagers hardly have time to take a break and have fun with their friends.
>
> On top of the demands from school, the attitudes of demanding parents often do not help. The constant query of "Have you done your biology revision yet?" can only add to the stress and frustration of having to give up the opportunity of fun for more schoolwork.

The key point of the first paragraph is that schoolwork can prevent teenagers from enjoying themselves.

The key point of the second paragraph is how parents can put pressure on teenagers.

Another way of spotting where a new point starts is when you see <u>linking words and phrases</u>:

however   secondly   furthermore   on the other hand   in addition

Taxi! Follow that argument...

If you try to talk about the whole text in one go, you'll more than likely end up in a sticky mess on the floor. But if you break an argument down into its main points, you'll find it a lot easier to discuss how the writer makes their points and how effective they are — see next page...

Evaluating an Argument

Evaluating an argument means saying how <u>effective</u> it is. You need to say whether or not you think it will persuade the reader to agree with the writer, and why.

Say What's Good about the argument

1) It's <u>not enough</u> just to say an argument is good. You need to say <u>how</u> the writer makes their points and explain <u>why</u> they're effective.

2) Think about what kind of <u>impression</u> (e.g. forceful, emotional, knowledgeable) the writer creates with the language they use, and <u>how</u> this impression helps to <u>persuade</u> the reader.

Unfortunately this isn't the key to a good answer.

Evaluate an argument Like This

Talk about one technique at a time.

> One reason that the argument is effective is the writer's use of adjectives. For example, negative words such as "stressful" are used to describe the difficulties teenagers face. These adjectives show that students find the amount of schoolwork difficult to cope with.

Give an example.

Say why the technique is effective.

The argument might have some Drawbacks

You might think some parts of an argument aren't convincing, and if that's what you reckon, <u>say so</u>. But if you do say this, make sure you've got some darn good <u>reasons</u> for saying so — if you just say, "the writer's argument is really stupid, he's missed the point", you won't get good marks.

Here are some criticisms you might be able to make:

1) <u>Confusing writing</u> — a writer might say things which <u>contradict</u> each other.

2) <u>Inaccurate information</u> — the writer's information might just be plain <u>wrong</u>. Watch out though — you have to be sure you really know your stuff before you go saying something's wrong.

3) <u>Dullness</u> — sometimes an argument just won't grab you. This might be because it's <u>full of statistics</u> and not much else, or because the text is <u>repetitive</u> or <u>unclear</u>. As always, if you can give examples of this, you'll pick up marks.

It was terrible! It wasn't that bad! It was great! MORE!

In your exam, you might be given a text that's presenting an argument. You need to be able to analyse the text by evaluating the argument and saying how successful it is. It's usually easiest to say mostly good things, but try to include one or two criticisms too, to make your answer balanced.

Facts

In your exam, it'll be useful if you can <u>spot facts and opinions</u> in texts and say what <u>effect</u> they have. Best get your head around the <u>difference</u> between them then...

Facts are definitely True...

> **FACT:** Manchester United won the UEFA Champions League in May 2008.
>
> **FACT:** Barack Obama was the President of the United States after George W. Bush.

...apart from False Facts — they're Untrue

My degree in accountancy really helped me further my career at Oceanworld.

> **FALSE FACT:** My nose is fifteen centimetres long.
>
> **FALSE FACT:** Madonna's real name is Derek Tyson.

Write about facts Like This

> The author uses facts in the text to strengthen his argument that Carl Lewis is the greatest sprinter and long jumper in history. For example, he mentions Lewis's nine Olympic gold medals, two world records for the 100 metres, and 65 consecutive long jump competition victories. Each fact proves the author's point about how successful Lewis was.

Make your point.

You could use "for example" to start your examples.

Explain why the author has used facts.

Not like this

<u>Don't</u> just count the facts and say where they are. It's a <u>classic mistake</u>. Don't do it.

> The author uses four facts in this text. There are two on line 2 and another two on line 5.

This answer doesn't say how the facts help the writer's argument.

FACT — gorillas are hairier than slugs...

...except bald gorillas of course. Anyway, make sure you can spot the facts in a piece of text, and say how the author uses them to get their point across. Then go and shave a gorilla.

Opinions

Now you know a bit about facts, it's time for <u>opinions</u>.

Opinions aren't True or Untrue — they're just Beliefs

Opinions are just what someone <u>thinks</u>. You <u>can't prove</u> that an opinion is true or untrue.

The words "I think" show that this is just a point of view.

OPINION: I think that animal testing for cosmetics should be banned.
OPINION: CD singles won't exist in 10 years' time.

You can't prove this one way or the other yet, even though it sounds like a fact.

Some sentences contain both Opinions AND Facts

Sometimes you can get opinions and facts in the <u>same sentence</u>. Like this one:

FACT AND OPINION: Manchester United gloriously won the UEFA Champions League in May 2008.

The word "gloriously" is just an opinion...

...but the second bit is fact.

This kind of writing is often a <u>sign of bias</u>.
Read more about bias on page 17.

Some people's opinions are more persuasive because they have a reputation for knowing a lot about a subject. E.g. When Jeremy Clarkson says he thinks some Vauxhalls are dull, people might see his opinion as fact, because he's thought of as a car expert.

Rah rah rah, everyone should get a car like MINE...

Write about Opinions Like This

Mention the effect the opinions have.

> The author uses strongly-worded opinions to mock people she does not like. For example: "Jamie Pullan comes second only to my three year old nephew in the contest for the World's most irritating display of chirpiness." The humour of these opinions creates an image in the reader's mind, making the author's argument more persuasive.

Explain why the author has used opinions.

In my opinion, Hugh Jackman is extremely good-looking...

If a text gives different opinions, you might need to compare them. There are a few phrases that often come in handy for this. Here's a few: similar to, contrasting with, on the other hand, different from, however, in agreement with, unlike, in the same way, conversely. All very useful.

Rhetoric

Rhetoric is when writers use <u>techniques</u> to make language more <u>persuasive</u> and <u>convincing</u>. The idea is to persuade their audience that there is only one sensible viewpoint — theirs.

Rhetorical Questions don't need an answer

1) Rhetorical questions are phrased to make the answer seem so <u>obvious</u> it's not even worth saying.
2) This makes the reader feel like they're <u>making their own mind up</u>, when actually the writer is deliberately trying to get them to think a <u>certain way</u>.

 Can it really be fair to set students these ridiculous and unnecessary assignments?

The words "ridiculous" and "unnecessary" are put there to get the reader to think, "No, of course it's not fair."

Repetition emphasises key points

1) Writers <u>repeat</u> words or phrases to <u>emphasise</u> their most important points.
2) They're often repeated in <u>threes</u>.

e.g. It's <u>outrageous</u> to suggest that pupils don't work hard. It's <u>outrageous</u> to suggest that we should give up all our free time for study. Most of all though, it's <u>outrageous</u> to expect us to take on even more homework.

Write about rhetoric Like This

As always, make a <u>point</u>, give an <u>example</u>, and explain the <u>effect</u>.

Say what effect the repeated word has — don't assume it's obvious.

The writer uses rhetoric to persuade the reader that students should not be given more homework to do. For example, his repetition of the word "outrageous" emphasises how awful more homework would be.

Exams are great, exams are great, exams are great...

There are lots of other <u>rhetorical techniques</u>, for example using emotive language (see page 31) or implications (suggesting something without saying it outright) to add to the text's impact.

Bias

If a text is biased, it <u>doesn't</u> give a <u>balanced</u> view. The writer's own point of view affects the writing.

Biased Writing is affected by the writer's opinions

1) Biased writers don't usually lie, but they <u>don't give the full picture</u>.

2) Sometimes the writer <u>exaggerates</u> something that supports their argument, or <u>doesn't mention</u> something that opposes it.

3) Bias <u>isn't always obvious</u>. The writing might have a formal, impersonal tone — but could still be influenced by the writer's opinions.

4) You need to be able to <u>recognise</u> bias, so that you don't mistake opinion for fact.

Bias looks like this

> Coldplay are the best band to come out of this country since the Beatles. They have produced hit after hit, and perform to huge sell-out crowds. Their music grabs you immediately and gets better with every listen.

Jim Dodd and the Budgies — stiff competition.

1) The text above <u>ignores</u> the fact that many other bands have lots of hits and play to big audiences.

2) There's <u>no hard evidence</u> there — no facts and figures to back up the writer's claims.

3) The last sentence is just <u>opinion</u> — lots of people might completely <u>disagree</u> with this.

Write about bias Like This

Make a clear opening point.

Say what the overall effect of the bias is.

The writer is clearly biased in favour of Coldplay. He mentions "hit after hit" and "huge sell-out crowds", but does not give any details. This clear bias makes the writer's argument less convincing as he appears to have made his opinion without finding any proper evidence for it.

Support it with quotes.

We're too expensive for you — you'll never bias...

A good way to spot bias is when the writer presents their opinion as fact, e.g. by saying something confidently but giving no evidence for it. This weakens their argument, as you can claim all sorts of absurd things this way — only yesterday someone tried to tell me that the moon's made of cheese.

Headlines

Presentational devices are used to make texts look more interesting.
Examples include: headlines, subheadings, numbered lists, columns, colour and pictures.

Headlines grab your Attention

1) Headlines tell you, very briefly, <u>what</u> an article is <u>about</u>.

2) In newspapers and magazines, headlines are always <u>bigger</u> than all the other words, and are at the <u>top</u> of the page.

3) The point of headlines is to capture your <u>interest</u>, so you'll read the article.

4) Headlines sometimes use <u>humour</u>, <u>exaggeration</u> or <u>shocking facts</u> to grab your attention.

Headlines look like this

These bits are the headlines.

Write about headlines Like This

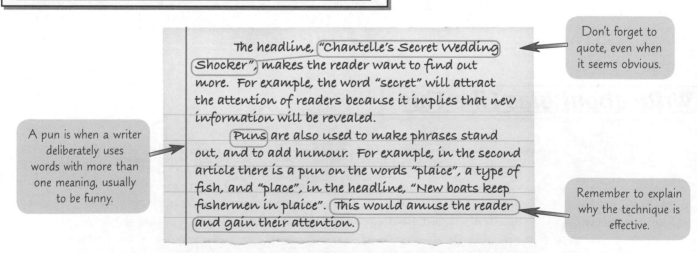

The headline, "Chantelle's Secret Wedding Shocker", makes the reader want to find out more. For example, the word "secret" will attract the attention of readers because it implies that new information will be revealed.

Puns are also used to make phrases stand out, and to add humour. For example, in the second article there is a pun on the words "plaice", a type of fish, and "place", in the headline, "New boats keep fishermen in plaice". This would amuse the reader and gain their attention.

Don't forget to quote, even when it seems obvious.

A pun is when a writer deliberately uses words with more than one meaning, usually to be funny.

Remember to explain why the technique is effective.

CGP Office Invaded by Dog in Pet Escape Scandal...

Headlines are there to attract your attention, so on some newspapers they're really big. If the headline's about something really exciting, it could be three inches tall — this makes it really stand out against its competitors on the newspaper stand when people are deciding which paper to buy.

Subheadings and Straplines

Subheadings and straplines are a bit like headlines, but, well, a bit different too. Read on.

Subheadings and Straplines help Organise the text

Subheadings

1) <u>Subheadings</u> are used to <u>split</u> the story up into little pieces to make it <u>easier to read</u>.

2) Each subheading briefly tells you <u>what</u> the next section of text is about.

3) They're usually a bit <u>bigger</u> than the rest of the text and might be <u>bold</u> or <u>underlined</u> to make them stand out.

Straplines

1) <u>Straplines</u> are short statements just <u>below</u> the headline.

2) The text is <u>smaller</u> than the headline but <u>bigger</u> than the main text.

3) The strapline tries to <u>keep the reader's interest</u> with a bit of extra info after the headline.

Subheadings and Straplines look like this

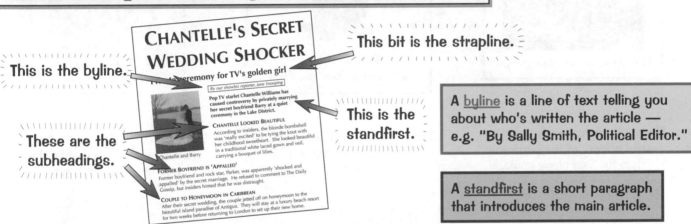

This is the byline.

This bit is the strapline.

This is the standfirst.

These are the subheadings.

A <u>byline</u> is a line of text telling you about who's written the article — e.g. "By Sally Smith, Political Editor."

A <u>standfirst</u> is a short paragraph that introduces the main article.

Write about subheadings and straplines Like This

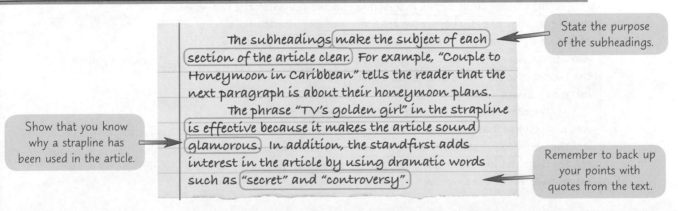

The subheadings make the subject of each section of the article clear. For example, "Couple to Honeymoon in Caribbean" tells the reader that the next paragraph is about their honeymoon plans.
The phrase "TV's golden girl" in the strapline is effective because it makes the article sound glamorous. In addition, the standfirst adds interest in the article by using dramatic words such as "secret" and "controversy".

State the purpose of the subheadings.

Show that you know why a strapline has been used in the article.

Remember to back up your points with quotes from the text.

Subheadings — send in the substitute headteacher...

Remember — don't just say what the subheading or strapline is. Anyone can do that. Make sure, instead, that you write about the choice of words and most importantly, their effect on the reader. It's not hard, this stuff, but you'll lose marks if you don't give examples and explain your points.

Graphics and Captions

"Graphics" is just a posh word for <u>pictures</u>. Graphics are often used to grab the reader's attention, back up the information in the text and make the meaning of the text clearer.

Graphics and Captions give us lots of Information

1) Texts often have graphics, e.g. photos, illustrations, diagrams, graphs and charts, to <u>show what they're about</u>.

2) They usually have <u>captions</u> with them — a short bit of text to explain what the graphic shows.

Graphics and Captions look like this

Hurricane causes devastation

The photo shows more about the awful effects of the hurricane than the text alone could.

A lifetime of fun and affection — take me home

This picture is persuasive — the cute puppy is meant to make the reader feel a bit soppy.

Friday, 9.00am

The caption clarifies what's being shown — it tells you when the weather forecast is for.

Write about graphics and captions Like This

The photograph of the hurricane shows us what the article is about, even before we read any of the words. It is effective because it is easy to understand quickly and makes us want to know more. For example, the picture of the hurricane damage shows us exactly how powerful the hurricane was.

The caption, "Hurricane causes devastation", tells us not only what happened, but also how we should feel about it. The word "devastation" in particular stresses to the reader that the hurricane would have been an awful experience for those involved.

State the purpose of the photo.

Say why it's effective.

Show how effective the caption is by describing its effect on the reader.

Think about why a particular picture's been used...

Remember, the graphic always goes with the words in the article. It shows us what the article is about. Don't just say what the graphic is, say <u>why</u> it's effective and how it connects to the text.

Text Columns

Text columns make the text easier to read and help to stop the reader getting confused.

Text can be Broken Up into Columns

1) Writers don't want you to get <u>bored</u> or <u>confused</u>, so they often break their text
    up into columns — it makes it appear shorter and <u>easier to read</u>.

2) Columns can also make certain bits of text <u>easier to find</u>.

3) You see <u>text columns</u> all over the place — in magazines, newspapers, adverts etc.

Columns look like this

Here's an example you might see in a <u>newspaper</u> or <u>magazine</u>.

These columns make the text look shorter and easy to read.

Different topics can be separated into different columns too.

Write about text columns Like This

> The writer has used text columns to make the text in the newspaper article appear easy to follow. Arranging the text in this way gives the impression that there is less text to read, and is therefore more reader-friendly than one big chunk of text.

Show you understand the effect of the text columns.

Text columns — ooh, how exciting...

If you don't really get it, just think about a newspaper without the columns. Imagine that all the writing just went from left to right in a giant block across the page. It'd be daunting to read — people would be scared away by the amount of text. Columns are a clever little trick really.

Bullet Points and Numbered Lists

Now that you understand how text columns work, it's time to look at other devices that writers use to make sure their work is clearly presented and easy to understand.

Bullet Points and Numbered Lists break texts down

1) <u>Bullet points</u> are <u>dots</u>, <u>dashes</u> or other <u>symbols</u> that go at the start of each new point in a <u>list</u>.

2) Sometimes lists can be <u>numbered</u> instead.

3) Bullet points and numbered lists are often used when writers want to give you <u>lots of information</u>. They separate information into <u>step-by-step</u> points, to make it <u>easier to read</u>.

Bullet Points and Numbered Lists look like this

I'm sure there was something I had to do today...

Learning to scuba dive involves:

- Equipment care
- Breathing from a regulator
- Caring for the environment
- Being safe

Dots are often used as bullet points.

Before your exam make sure that you:

1. Know where and when the exam is.
2. Get a good night's sleep.
3. Get up in time to have breakfast.
4. Have everything you need for the exam.

This is a numbered list.

Tracy had forgotten point 5 — do the exam.

Write about bullet points and numbered lists Like This

Show you know that the writer has thought carefully about how to present the text.

The writer has chosen to summarise what you might learn in a scuba diving course by using bullet points. This is an effective way of presenting a large amount of information, as it breaks the points down, making them easier to follow.

In the second example, the writer presents his advice as a numbered list. The use of numbers emphasises the order in which the advice should be followed. It also reassures the reader by giving the impression that there is only a limited amount of information to remember.

Show you know what effect bullet points have on the reader.

Show you understand that the numbers are there for a reason.

My bullet points didn't work — they must've been blanks...

OK, it doesn't take a genius to spot a bullet point, but it's still worth writing about them. Show the examiner that you understand the effect different ways of presenting text can have on the reader, and you can get yourself a couple of extra marks — which is always nice.

Colour

"Wow, look at all the colours!" said Bob Grey the boredom inspector. "Grey, brown, beige... cream! It's all too exciting. I think I need a lie down."

Colour affects how you Read a text

1) The colour of the lettering or background can affect how we read a text.

2) Writers know this, which means that when they use colours, they want a particular effect.

3) For example, lots of bright colours could suggest that an article is about a fun topic, like dancing, while dark colours might be used to create a serious mood for an article about war.

Colour is Used like this

Real-life stories

Blah blah de darr blah dhjt gobbledy gook. Blah basl de darr blah gobbledy xfdgy gook. Blah blah de darr blah gobbledy gook. Ab blah blah de darr blah fergki bloh gobbledy gook. Blah bl frd de darr blah gobbledy tgjj Blah blah de darr
De darr blah fergki bloh gobbledy gook. Blah bl frd de darr blah gobbledy tgjj Blah blah de darr blah erx

This is no ordinary tiger — it's my new husband!

frljn lah blah de darr blah dh sgge gobbledy gook. Blah ba de darr blah gobbledy xdfdgy gook. Blah blah de da dad r¹ ¹¹³h gobbledy gook ¹ darr ¹¹

frljn lah blah de darr blah dh sgge gobbledy gook. Blah ba de darr blah gobbledy xdfdgy ¹¹³h blah. ¹¹, ø¹

frljn lah blah de darr blah dj sgge gobbledy gook. Blah sl ¹¹hbbledy xdfdgy ¹¹¹ a

This page has an orange colour scheme. It suits the topic of tigers, and looks good as a whole with the tiger picture.

Heavenly Food
· Fruit
· Vegetables
· Nuts
· Whole grain cereal

Sinful food
· Chocolate
· Crisps
· Crisps
· D⁻⁻ fried

Different-coloured backgrounds are used to create a contrast between "heavenly" and "sinful" foods.

Write about colour Like This

Colours have been used to create a contrast between "heavenly" and "sinful" foods. The heavenly side has been given light, pure-looking colours, which add to the heavenly theme and make the reader feel relaxed. The sinful side is red, which creates a sense of danger, making the reader feel tense and uneasy.

Show that you understand how colour can be used to exaggerate differences.

Show that you understand the effect of colour on the reader.

Sadly there isn't a "colouring in" part of the exam...

Sometimes colour is used to draw your attention to something, but often it has more meaning. Traditionally, we associate red with danger, bright colours with excitement, and dull colours with boring or serious things. Also look out for contrasting colours which often emphasise a difference.

Font Styles

Everything on a page tells you something about the text. This includes what the writing looks like.

Fonts are different Styles of printed text

The mischievous smile meant she'd written her speech in Litterbox ICG again.

1) The <u>font</u> of a text gives you a clue about <u>what kind</u> of text it is.
2) Serious, formal fonts are for <u>serious</u>, formal texts.
3) Cartoony, childish fonts are for <u>light-hearted</u> texts, or texts for <u>children</u>.

Here are some examples of Different Fonts

There will be a community watch meeting at the village hall on Sunday.

- Look how formal and serious this font is.

There will be a brownie/ scout meeting at the village hall on Sunday.

- This font is clear and easy to read, without being too official-looking.

There will be a drama club meeting at the village hall on Sunday.

- This font is harder to read, but looks impressive and arty.

Write about font style Like This

The writers use font styles that are appropriate for the subject matter and audience. The font in the first example is quite traditional and formal. For this reason, it might appeal to an older audience, who are the people most likely to attend the "community watch meeting" being advertised.
The type of font in the second text, as in the first, is suitable for its intended audience. A font that looks like a child's writing has been used to advertise a "brownie/scout meeting". The informal, friendly font has been chosen in order to appeal to children who might be interested in this event.

State what kind of audience the font will appeal to.

Show that you can see the similarities and differences between texts.

You don't need to know the names of the fonts — just describe them.

The best font is ZapfDingbats — ✔•✚✳❋○■◆○❂✳□✖…

Remember, the font tells you about the tone of the text at first glance. So a serious, boring font tells you that the text is probably very formal and is not a laughing matter. A silly, cartoony font tells you that the text is light-hearted, jokey and informal. It's not rocket science, this font stuff.

Font Formatting

Formatting means making words or sentences stand out from the rest of the text, for example by making them **bold** or *italic*, underlining them or putting them in CAPITALS.

Fonts can be Formatted to create different Effects

1) Different styles of the same font have different effects on the reader.
2) Writers format fonts to emphasise particular words or phrases and make them really stand out.
3) To do this, they make them look different from the rest of the text.

Formatting looks like this

Bold is useful for highlighting important words.

Capital letters are often used for headings.

WOMEN SWIM INTO RECORD BOOKS

At 10pm last night, the last of the **5,000** female swimmers arrived at Calais, having set off from Dover at 5am. This marks the largest group swim ever in the history of swimming.

The women together have raised over **a million pounds** for a variety of charities. They plan to repeat the event next year, and hopefully double their numbers.

The event's organiser, Gill Potts said, *"I'm really pleased with everyone's effort. They had to swim through two miles of jellyfish, but not one of them complained."*

Waiting at Calais was Robbie Williams, who had promised a **kiss** for each swimmer to arrive. When told that 5,000 women were approaching the shore, the singer was apparently *"a little shocked"*.

Could you swim the channel? Visit www.swimmingisgreat.org for details on next year's event.

Italics can be used to highlight quotes.

Underlining can be used to highlight important words and website addresses.

Write about formatting Like This

One of the writer's intentions is to make the readers realise how many people took part in the swim, and how much money they raised for charity. This is made really clear as "5,000" and "a million pounds" are printed in bold, making these words stand out from the rest so that the reader cannot miss them.

Show that you know the writer has used bold formatting on purpose.

Remember to mention the effect on the reader.

I'd like to do some formatting, if I may be so bold...

When you are comparing how pieces of text are presented, write about the differences and similarities in the font style and formatting. But make sure you remember to write about the effects that these different styles of font have on the readers too. That's the only way to get decent marks.

Descriptive Language

The texts you have to write about in the exam will use lots of different language techniques to make them more effective. You need to be able to recognise the techniques and say why they're used.

Descriptive Language makes text Interesting

1) <u>Descriptive language</u> includes <u>imagery</u> such as metaphors, similes and personification (see page 27).

2) Writers often give <u>descriptions</u> based on their five <u>senses</u>.

3) Another sign of descriptive language is when the writer uses lots of <u>adjectives</u> — describing words like "huge" or "fiery".

4) Descriptive language creates a <u>picture</u> in the reader's mind. It also makes the text more <u>interesting</u>, <u>dramatic</u> and <u>real</u>.

- what they can <u>see</u>
- what they can <u>smell</u>
- what they can <u>hear</u>
- what they can <u>feel</u> or <u>touch</u>
- what they can <u>taste</u>

EXAMPLE After the dreary, grey sheet of rain had swept over the land, the parched, sun-baked fields transformed into a fertile, emerald-green valley.

Write about descriptive language Like This

This answer uses P.E.E. (see p.35)

The writer uses descriptive language to describe the effect of the rains on the African landscape. He uses adjectives such as "parched" and "sun-baked" to describe the dry fields before the rain and contrasts them with the bright "emerald-green valley" after the rain. This allows the reader to picture how dramatic the changes that the rains bring are.

Here are your examples.

Explain <u>why</u> the writer has used descriptive language.

Don't do it like this

The writer uses lots of descriptive language which makes it more interesting.

Don't just say it makes it more interesting.

To get the marks, you need to say <u>why</u> the descriptive language makes the text more interesting for the reader.

Dave tried desperately to cool down his Potentially Explosive Elephant so he could use him in more exam answers.

My dad used descriptive language when I broke his mug...

It's not too hard to get the hang of writing about these techniques — just spot where one's been used, quote it, and explain how it's been used deliberately to affect the reader in some way. Easy.

Metaphors, Similes and Personification

Metaphors, similes and personification are all types of <u>imagery</u> (see glossary).

Metaphors, similes and personification are Comparisons

Metaphors, similes and personification describe one thing by <u>comparing</u> it to something else.

<u>Metaphors</u> describe something by saying that it <u>is</u> something else.

> **EXAMPLE** I tried to run but my feet <u>were</u> blocks of concrete.

<u>Similes</u> describe something by saying that it's <u>like</u> something else. They usually use the words <u>as</u> or <u>like</u>.

> **EXAMPLE** The humid Italian air clings to my skin <u>like</u> a warm, wet blanket.

<u>Personification</u> means describing something <u>as if it's a person</u> or an <u>animal</u>.

> **EXAMPLE** The helicopter's menacing <u>growl</u> frightened the crowd.

Write about metaphors Like This

Here's your point, made right at the start of your paragraph.

Here's your example.

Here's your explanation.

The journalist uses a metaphor when reporting from the war zone, "I tried to run but my feet were blocks of concrete". This direct comparison gives the reader a sense of the situation being so frightening that he could not even move to run away.

Write about similes Like This

This quote is tucked neatly into the sentence.

By using the simile "like a warm, wet blanket" to describe the Italian air, the reader can really feel just how unpleasantly damp and sticky the air is.

Write about personification Like This

Say what impression the personification creates.

Use quotes to back up your points.

The writer's use of personification makes the helicopter appear threatening. Describing it as having a "menacing growl" makes it sound like a dangerous wild animal.

The spectre of the exam lurked like an invisible tiger...

Metaphors — his breath was ice, my boss is a pussycat really, your trainers are pure cheese.
Similes — his breath was as cold as ice, my boss is as nice as a cat, your trainers smell like cheese.

Alliteration and Onomatopoeia

Alliteration and onomatopoeia are used as sound effects in writing to keep readers interested.

Alliteration means repeating the same Sound

Alliteration is when words that are close together begin with the same sound. It makes the sentence seem more interesting to the reader. Alliteration is often found in headlines:

P.M.'s Panic
Rooney Rules the Roost
Close Call for Kids
Magic Murray Marches On

In the exam you'll need to identify alliteration and write about how and why it's been used.

Write about alliteration Like This

The alliteration of "Magic Murray Marches On" attracts the reader's attention to the article on Andy Murray at Wimbledon. Alliteration emphasises the headline and gives the article a snappy opening which adds to the reader's interest.

Here's the example.

Don't forget to expand your explanation to describe the effects on the reader.

Onomatopoeia means words that Imitate Noises

Onomatopoeia means words that sound like the noises being described. This makes the description of the sounds more effective. Here are some good examples:

Thud   Slurp   Crackle   Smash   Tinkle   Screech   Hiss   Squish

Write about onomatopoeia Like This

Remember the effect on the reader.

The onomatopoeia of "slurp" in the cartoon used in the milkshake advertisement makes the audience recognise the humorous noise often made by children when they drink. This makes the product seem more fun and appealing to the children the text is aimed at.

Here's the example.

Think about the purpose of the text when you're writing about onomatopoeia.

Onomatopoeia — what a stupid word...

Learn how to spell ON-O-MAT-O-POEI-A. You'll impress the examiner if you can spell it correctly. It's hard, I know, but just write it out a few times and you'll get the hang of it eventually.

Irony and Sarcasm

Irony and sarcasm are techniques that are related to the <u>tone</u> of the writing (see glossary).

Irony is saying the Opposite of what you Mean

1) <u>Irony</u> is when someone <u>says one thing</u>, but <u>means</u> the <u>opposite</u>.
2) Irony is often <u>humorous</u> or <u>light-hearted</u>.

> **EXAMPLE** We were stranded at the airport for 48 hours with no food, which was just great.

Of course, the writer doesn't <u>really</u> mean it was great. In fact, he means it was the <u>opposite</u> of great.

Write about irony Like This

Here's your point. Say <u>why</u> the writer has used irony.

The writer uses irony to express his frustration at having his flight delayed. When he says that being there for 48 hours with no food was "just great" he actually means the opposite — the lack of food clearly added to his irritation.

Here's your explanation.

Sarcasm is Nastier than irony

1) <u>Sarcasm</u> is language that has a <u>mocking</u> or <u>scornful</u> tone.
2) It's often intended to <u>insult a person</u> or <u>make fun</u> of them, or to show that the writer is <u>angry</u> about something.
3) Sarcastic writing often uses <u>irony</u> — but the tone is more <u>aggressive</u> and <u>unpleasant</u>.

> **EXAMPLE** The council's latest brainwave on tackling petty crime is to take away the few local facilities available to youngsters. This is presumably intended to encourage them to stay indoors watching Hollyoaks rather than engaging with society in any way.

Write about sarcasm Like This

The writer's use of sarcasm in describing the council's "brainwave" shows how stupid he thinks it is. His sarcastic comment that it is "presumably intended" to exclude young people from society suggests that the council have not thought it through.

Explain the intended effect of the sarcasm.

Sarcasm, yeah right, what a great technique...

Keep a look out for irony and sarcasm in the reading texts. If a writer says something like, "I just love waiting in long queues to buy mouldy, out-of-date yoghurt", you shouldn't take them literally.

Technical Language

Some of the texts in the exam might contain some technical language. This can be used to make the writer sound knowledgeable about the subject, or just to add detail to the text.

Technical language is often used to Support an argument

1) <u>Technical</u> language includes things like <u>specialist terms</u> and <u>statistics</u>.

2) Technical language gives an impression of the writer having <u>in-depth knowledge</u> of the topic they're writing about. This can make their arguments <u>more convincing</u>.

3) You'll find technical language in <u>textbooks</u>, <u>instructions</u>, <u>reports</u>, and <u>newspaper articles</u>.

"Nope, I don't understand what 'inter-departmental rationalising' means either. It must be good though."

Technical Language looks like this

> Governments need to act now in order to combat climate change. Average worldwide temperatures have increased by about 1°C in the last hundred years, mainly due to increased emission of greenhouse gases such as carbon dioxide and methane.

Facts and statistics are used.

Specialist terms.

Write about technical language Like This

As always, remember to talk about the <u>effect</u> of the type of language you're writing about — think about the <u>impression</u> the writer is after.

> By including technical terms relating to climate change, such as "average worldwide temperatures" and "greenhouse gases", the writer gives the impression that he understands the more complex details of the issue. He seems to know the exact nature of the problems, and this supports his argument that governments need to take more action to deal with climate change.

You won't pick up many marks if you forget to quote.

Explain how technical language makes the writer's argument more convincing.

Here comes the science...

There's nothing here that's too hard to get your head around. You don't have to know what all the technical language means — just say what impression it creates. It can be used to give detail, but more often than not it's there to make the author sound like they know what they're on about.

Emotive Language

Emotive language appeals to your emotions, to try to get you to feel something, e.g. anger, fear or happiness.

Emotive language is used to Persuade

1) Writers use emotive language to get the reader to <u>feel</u> really <u>strongly</u> about something.

2) This could be feelings of disgust, sadness, happiness, anger or any other <u>emotion</u>.

3) Language is often made emotive by <u>strong adjectives</u>, e.g. "shocking", "shameful" or "heroic".

4) <u>Emotive</u> language can <u>emphasise</u> a point — it usually makes the <u>writer's opinion</u> very clear.

5) <u>Tabloid newspapers</u> often use emotive language to interest their readers (see p.32).

Sophie felt emotional after reading 'Spot the Dog'.

Emotive Language looks like this

The bears are forced to perform these painful dances and are frequently subjected to physical abuse. But by supporting our organisation, you can help to save these gentle, innocent creatures and put an end to this shameful and mindless cruelty once and for all.

Words like "painful" and "abuse" encourage the reader to feel upset about how the bears are treated.

Write about emotive language Like This

Make a simple opening point to show what you're talking about.

The leaflet against animal cruelty uses very emotive language. The words "forced" and "painful" are used to affect the reader's emotions, persuading them to feel that this treatment is cruel and unacceptable.

Explain the effect of the emotive language on the reader.

Emotive — not "a reason for having the internet"...

So emotive language makes you emotional — tricky eh? Writers use it because making the reader feel guilty or sad is sometimes a more effective way of <u>persuading</u> them than just bombarding them with statistics. It's persuasive because it makes the reader feel more <u>personally involved</u>.

Tabloid Newspaper Language

There are masses of features you can talk about if you get a tabloid newspaper article in the exam.

Tabloids use a Specific Style of language

Tabloid newspapers, e.g. The Sun and The News of the World, are small, almost square-shaped and usually have big headlines, photos and opinionated articles. They're less serious than broadsheet newspapers like 'The Times'. Here are some examples of tabloid newspaper style, or "tabloidese" as it's sometimes called:

Nicknames are used to make the reader feel they know someone well. They're most often used for celebrities.

> Examples include: "Fergie", "Posh and Becks", "Princess Di".

Slang words, informal language and short, simple sentences are used to make the readers feel that the newspaper is chatting to them.

> Examples include: "soap stars in spat", "we won a whopping £30 million", "celebs".

Puns and wordplay are used to make the newspaper seem jokey and fun.

> Examples include: "Sven's he going?", "Brad's the Pitts".

Tabloid Style looks like this

FRANKIE FANS THE FLAMES

By our sports writer, Rick Roberts

Hopping-mad Wabbingford City manager Sid Franklin has lashed out at striker Ruud Van der Livary after his Wednesday walkout.

Fed up Frankie blasted the player after he turned down a new contract for a megabucks deal at French side FC Montjoi.

Ruud awakening

"Obviously our offer wasn't good enough," Frankie fumed. "I'm gutted but I'll accept it because I only want players who are committed, not greedy money-grabbers."

Write about tabloid journalism Like This

The alliteration of "Frankie Fans the Flames" in the headline grabs the reader's attention. The use of the nickname "Frankie" suggests that the article has inside information, as it gives the impression that the writer knows the person involved.
Puns and slang expressions are used throughout the article. For example, "Ruud awakening" uses a play on words with the player's name and the word "rude". This creates a light-hearted tone and keeps the reader amused.

> Use the right terms.

> Say why the newspaper has used this technique.

> Keep referring closely to the text and you'll get the marks.

I just can't stand all those puns that tabloids use...

I bet you thought GCSE English would be all Shakespeare and poetry. Nope, you get to read all the latest hot gossip about badly behaved footballers and celebrity romances too. Lucky you.

Structure

"Structure" means the way different parts of a text are put together.

Introductions create Interest in the text

1) An introduction should <u>briefly</u> give the reader the <u>main points</u> of the article.
2) It should also <u>interest</u> the reader enough to read the <u>rest</u> of the article.

e.g. Fears were voiced last night for the safety of the lone whale who was spotted in the Thames by the Embankment in Central London. Onlookers have nicknamed him "Willy" and have taken to the banks of the river to watch.

Emotive language makes the reader want to find out more.

Gives the main points.

Write about introductions Like This

Make your point straight away.

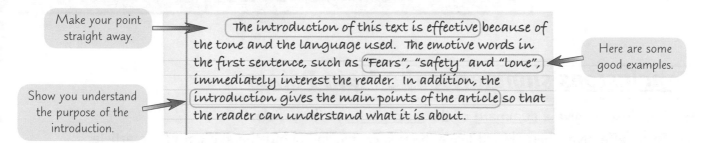

The introduction of this text is effective because of the tone and the language used. The emotive words in the first sentence, such as "Fears", "safety" and "Lone", immediately interest the reader. In addition, the introduction gives the main points of the article so that the reader can understand what it is about.

Here are some good examples.

Show you understand the purpose of the introduction.

The middle tells you Who, What, Where, When and Why

After the introduction, the main bit of text gives the reader some <u>details</u> about the story.

Nathan and his team were trying to figure out who, what, where, when and why.

e.g.

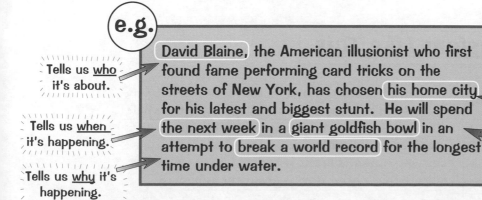

David Blaine, the American illusionist who first found fame performing card tricks on the streets of New York, has chosen his home city for his latest and biggest stunt. He will spend the next week in a giant goldfish bowl in an attempt to break a world record for the longest time under water.

Tells us <u>who</u> it's about.

Tells us <u>when</u> it's happening.

Tells us <u>why</u> it's happening.

Tells us <u>where</u> it's happening.

Tells us <u>what</u> is going on.

Who? What? Where? Nurse, the pills...

This is all fairly obvious really — the introduction gives a general idea of what's in the article, then you get the details. The next page shows you how these details are structured in the main text, before it's all nicely summed up in the conclusion. And they all lived happily ever after...

Structure

The middle of the article gives more details about the facts described in the introduction. Then the conclusion sums everything up and leaves the reader with something to think about.

The Body of the text is usually Structured in Paragraphs

Here's one common way of structuring an article:

1) The <u>main points</u> of a text are first given very briefly in the <u>introduction</u>.

2) Each <u>paragraph</u> of the <u>main body</u> of the text then <u>expands</u> on these ideas in turn.

Here's the main body of the whale article from the previous page:

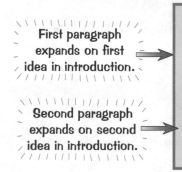

First paragraph expands on first idea in introduction.

Second paragraph expands on second idea in introduction.

> The whale, identified as a humpback that would normally be found in transatlantic waters, is bleeding from a wound to its side. It has been swimming alongside the Houses of Parliament all afternoon, having first been spotted by a French tourist who was walking the popular route.
> The number of onlookers has rapidly increased during the afternoon as news of Willy's sighting spread through the cafes, shops and offices of Central London. The crowd has been very considerate of the whale's welfare by maintaining a quiet presence.

Conclusions summarise the Main Points

1) Conclusions give a <u>summary</u> of the <u>main points</u> of the article.

2) To be effective, they should leave the reader <u>thinking</u> about the <u>subject</u> of the article.

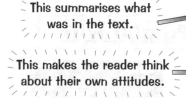

This summarises what was in the text.

This makes the reader think about their own attitudes.

> The questions that remain unanswered are how Willy came to be in the Thames and whether or not he will live. However, the most intriguing question is why are we, as humans, so interested in his plight?

Write about conclusions Like This

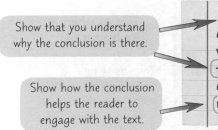

Show that you understand why the conclusion is there.

Show how the conclusion helps the reader to engage with the text.

The conclusion sums up the main points of the article, such as the concerns about whether the whale will survive or not. This emphasises the main points for the reader. In addition, the last sentence, which asks why humans are so interested, encourages the reader to think more deeply about the subject.

And in conclusion, this is all dead easy...

So let me get this straight — the introduction's at the start and the conclusion's at the end, you say? You're absolutely sure about that then? Well, it's crazy, but it just might work...

P.E.E.

P.E.E. is a great technique for getting <u>excellent marks</u>. Best learn how to do it then.

P.E.E. stands for Point Example Explanation

To write a good answer that gets you plenty of marks, you must do <u>three</u> things:

1) Make a <u>point</u> to answer the question you've been given.

2) Then give an <u>example</u> from the text (either a quote or a description).

3) After that, <u>explain</u> how your example backs up your point.

Here's an example answer that includes those <u>three</u> things:

This is your point.

This is your example, a quote from the text.

This bit is your explanation.

The writer feels quite angry about school dinners. She says school food is "pallid, tasteless pap". The word "pap" has a disgusted sound to it showing her opinion about the poor quality of the food.

P.E.E. is also called P.Q.D. (Point Quote Discuss),
P.Q.C. (Point Quote Comment)
or S.E.C. (Statement Example Comment).

Explain what your example Shows about the Text

1) Your example will usually be a <u>quote</u>, but it can also be a <u>reference</u>, e.g. a description of the pictures, font, layout or structure of the text.

2) The <u>explanation</u> part is very important. It's your chance to make your point <u>clear</u>.

Here are some answers with <u>different types of examples</u> and clear <u>explanations</u>:

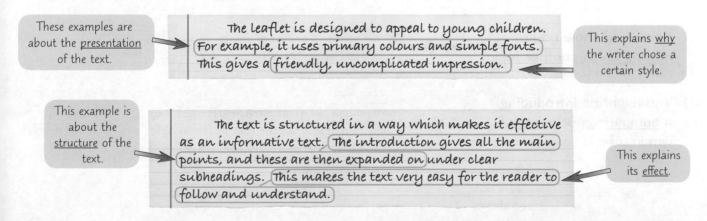

These examples are about the <u>presentation</u> of the text.

The leaflet is designed to appeal to young children. For example, it uses primary colours and simple fonts. This gives a friendly, uncomplicated impression.

This explains <u>why</u> the writer chose a certain style.

This example is about the <u>structure</u> of the text.

The text is structured in a way which makes it effective as an informative text. The introduction gives all the main points, and these are then expanded on under clear subheadings. This makes the text very easy for the reader to follow and understand.

This explains its <u>effect</u>.

Would you like to share the joke with the rest of the class?

P.E.E. might seem a bit dull, but it's a really solid way to craft your answers. For the longer, <u>higher-mark questions</u> you'll have to make <u>several points</u>. Make sure you back up each point with an example and an explanation (and remember to have a sly <u>giggle</u> or two over the word "PEE").

Writing in Paragraphs

You need to know <u>why</u> paragraphs are so important and how to <u>start</u> a good one.

Paragraphs are useful in the <u>Longer Questions</u>

1) For <u>higher-mark</u> questions, you've got to make <u>several detailed points</u>.

2) You need to <u>organise</u> your points clearly and <u>link</u> them together
— and the best way to do that is to write in <u>paragraphs</u>.

3) If a question's got <u>bullet points</u>, write at least <u>one paragraph</u> for each bullet point.

4) If there are <u>no</u> bullet points in the question, use a <u>paragraph</u> for each point in your answer.

> Each paragraph could be structured with <u>P.E.E.</u>
> (Point, Example, Explanation — see last page).

How you <u>Start</u> each New Paragraph <u>is important</u>

<u>Linking</u> your paragraphs together smoothly is an important skill — it makes your writing look <u>more confident</u> and <u>better thought out</u>.

1) The beginning of a paragraph needs to show <u>what</u> the paragraph is <u>about</u>. Link it to <u>key words</u> in the question.

> The writer creates an immediate sense of anger through the headlines she chooses.

This makes it clear you're answering a question about how the writer shows anger.

2) You might want to <u>link</u> a new point with a <u>previous paragraph</u>.

> This is not the only way in which the writer shows bias.

This refers back to the paragraph you've just finished.

3) You could show you're <u>moving on</u> to another topic.

> The writer's choice of fonts is also important.

This introduces your new topic.

4) You might be introducing a <u>comparison</u> or <u>contrast</u> within a text.

> Although the first paragraph uses lots of questions, the rest of the article sounds much more authoritative.

This word helps you start writing about a difference.

See page 12 for some more examples of linking words and phrases.

Make a chart of tropical birds — draw a parrotgraph...

This stuff kind of comes naturally when you've had enough practice. So keep doing practice exams and answering practice questions — pretty soon you'll be producing beautiful answers.

Reading with Insight

"Insight" means noticing the less obvious things about a text. It's very useful for the longer answers.

Think about the writer's Attitude and Motivation

1) You can show <u>insight</u> if you work out what a writer's <u>attitude</u> is. For example:

> There is a strong sense that the writer feels angry about the changes.

2) You could comment on how the writer tries to make readers <u>feel</u>. For example:

> The writer seems to want to make readers feel guilty.

3) You might write about <u>why</u> you think a piece was written. For example:

> Perhaps the writer felt he needed to make sure the memory of his friend was kept alive.

You need to look Beyond what's Obvious

Writers don't always make things obvious. You can use <u>evidence</u> in the text to work out what the writer <u>really</u> means. Make sure you use <u>details</u> from the text though. Don't just guess.

1) <u>Language</u> gives you clues.

> The writer uses words like "endless" and "glum". This implies that he did not enjoy the film.

> This phrase is useful for showing you've thought about what the writer really thinks.

2) <u>Pictures</u> with the text might give you some ideas.

> The article appears to be critical of the circus because it includes pictures of animals cramped in cages and fields full of litter.

3) The <u>content</u> of the text will give you hints.

> The writer gives the impression of being in favour of the exam system because she only uses examples of successful candidates.

The Examiner wants to hear Your Opinion

You can get marks for giving thoughtful <u>personal opinions</u>. Make sure you focus on the <u>text</u> though — examiners don't want to know your general opinions on various unrelated issues.

THIS WOULD BE GOOD:

> I think the article would remind older people of happier times because it includes so many descriptive details.

THIS WOULD BE BAD:

> I think old people are quite boring.

Make sure you're reading with insight of a cup of tea...

There's lots of really good advice on this page. I'd read it over one more time if I were you. Using some of these higher-level techniques will help you to achieve a 'C' grade in the exam.

Search and Find Questions

The simplest type of exam question asks you to pick out particular information from a text. Here are some tips on how to answer them well...

Some questions ask you to Pick Out Information

1) These questions test your ability to read and <u>understand</u> the text, then <u>select suitable information</u> from it.

2) Here's an example:

> Read **Item 1**, the article called *Homecoming* by Betty Munro.
> 1   Why is Melrose a wonderful place to live?
> *(4 marks)*

3) This type of question is fairly straightforward — but you need to make sure you find <u>all</u> the <u>relevant details</u> and write about them <u>clearly</u> to get <u>top marks</u>.

Read the text Carefully

1) After you've read the exam question, <u>look back through</u> the <u>text</u>.

2) As you read, <u>underline</u> information that <u>answers the question</u>.
E.g. here's part of the text that goes with the exam question above:

> At the age of 46, I was fed up of London. I sold my house and rented a cottage in the <u>idyllic</u> Scottish town where I grew up. After just a few weeks, I knew I'd made the right decision: Melrose, with its <u>friendly people</u> and <u>stunning scenery</u>, is where my heart is and it's a wonderful place to live.
> It is <u>terribly pretty</u>, with the kind of <u>charming</u>, local <u>shops</u> that are rapidly being replaced by supermarket giants elsewhere. For such a tiny place, it is <u>buzzing with life</u>. There's a <u>theatre</u>, <u>museum</u> and literary society. The <u>sporting facilities are fantastic</u>, with an <u>excellent rugby pitch</u>.

It's important to Keep your answer Focused

1) Select the parts of the text that <u>answer the question best</u> — don't include any extra waffle.

2) You can use <u>short quotes</u>, or explain what the writer says <u>in your own words</u>. If you use quotes, remember to use <u>quotation marks</u>.

3) Avoid quoting <u>long chunks</u> — it gives the examiner the impression that you <u>don't understand</u> the text and can't tell which bits are most important.

4) All the points you make should be <u>based on the text</u> and <u>help to answer the question</u>.

THIS WOULD BE GOOD:
> The writer says Melrose is "terribly pretty" and has "charming" shops. She is also enthusiastic about the sporting facilities, for example the "excellent" rugby field.

THIS WOULD BE BAD:
> The writer says that at the age of 46, she was fed up of London. She must have been bored of cities. She seems to think Melrose is much better than London, probably because it's rural.

Where could you find a question? — Search me....

With 'search and find' questions it's important to follow the text closely, and pick out all the relevant points. Don't get sidetracked. Save your skills of insight and evaluation for the trickier questions...

Comparing Texts

In the exam, there will be a question that asks you to <u>compare two texts</u>. For example, you might have to compare the way they are written or how they are presented. These questions can be tricky — so here's a page of hints about how to tackle them...

Plan your answer Before you start Writing

Here's a <u>question</u> that asks you to compare two texts:

> Now look again at all three items. They have each been written in an interesting way.
>
> 1   Choose **two** of these items. Compare them using these headings:
>   - the writers' intended audiences
>   - the ways in which the writers use language.

And here's how you could <u>plan</u> an answer to that question:

Set your notes out in lists, side by side, to help you compare.

Each set of notes matches a bullet point or key word in the question.

Item 1
- Audience — teenagers, because it uses informal font, cartoons
- Use of language — slang, enthusiastic tone, abbreviations, short sentences, jokes

Item 2
- Audience — adult readers, because it uses columns, small font
- Use of language — formal, critical, emotive language

Try to Compare the texts as you Go Along

Here's part of a <u>sample answer</u> to the question above. It's about the first bullet point (comparing "the writers' intended audiences"):

This introduces a difference.

> The author of Item 1 is writing for a teenage audience, whereas Item 2 is for adults. This is partly suggested by the appearance of each text. Item 1 uses an informal font and includes cartoons, which would appeal to young people. Item 2, on the other hand, is set out in traditional newspaper columns with a small font size, which suggests that it is aimed at adults.

The paragraph discusses <u>both</u> texts and compares them directly.

Next up, all the way from Bolton — oh you said "compare"

Make sure you include loads of cross-references — go back and forth between texts so that you're always <u>comparing</u>. Here are some words that'll help: "similarly", "despite", "in contrast to", "just as", "equally", "alternatively", "in the same way" and "likewise". Try to memorise a few of these.

SECTION FIVE — EXAM TECHNIQUES

Summary of the Exam

I bet you're just aching to know all about your exam. Well, the next two pages tell you what the exam's going to be like and how long you should spend on the different bits. Fun fun fun.

The Exam's in Two Sections

1) Whether you're doing <u>GCSE English Language</u> or <u>GCSE English</u>, you only have to do <u>one exam</u>.

2) It's the <u>same</u> exam for both courses, and it's for <u>Unit 1: Understanding and producing non-fiction texts</u>.

3) You get <u>2 hours 15 minutes</u> for the exam. Here's how it's <u>structured</u>:

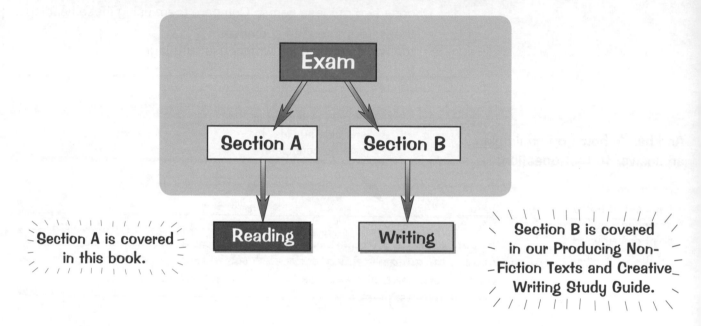

Section A is covered in this book.

Section B is covered in our Producing Non-Fiction Texts and Creative Writing Study Guide.

The Front Page tells you What To Do

First up — <u>what to do</u> when you plonk yourself down in that nice, comfy exam chair (there's more on the <u>structure</u> of the exam on the next page):

1) The <u>front page</u> of the exam paper tells you what you should have in front of you. Read it through and make sure you've <u>got everything</u>.

   • There will be a <u>main exam paper</u> which will have all the <u>questions</u> and <u>space</u> to write your <u>answers</u>.

   • You'll also have a <u>separate insert</u> containing <u>three non-fiction texts</u>.

2) Make sure you fill in all the <u>details</u> you're asked for on the <u>front</u> of the exam paper, or you won't get any marks at all — not ideal.

3) Make sure you've got the <u>foundation tier</u> paper, not the higher one.

4) Read all the <u>instructions and tips</u> on the front page, to remind you what to do.

My mum tells me what to do...

So there you are, one lovely exam on non-fiction texts and that's Unit 1 sorted. All we're looking at in this book is the first part of the exam (understanding non-fiction texts, also known as reading), but it's good to know a bit about the other part too (producing non-fiction texts, or writing).

Summary of the Exam

This page is about the different <u>questions</u>, and how many <u>marks</u> each one's worth. Crikey, with all this info to remember about the exam, they'll be giving you an exam on the exam next...

Section A and Section B are Both Worth 40 Marks

1) The whole exam is worth <u>80 marks</u>, and counts for <u>40%</u> of your total GCSE mark (for both GCSE English Language and GCSE English).

2) You can get up to <u>40 marks</u> for <u>Section A</u> and <u>40 marks</u> for <u>Section B</u>.

3) Section A will have <u>five</u> questions — <u>two</u> worth <u>4 marks</u>, <u>one</u> worth <u>8 marks</u> and <u>two</u> worth <u>12 marks</u>.

4) Section B will have <u>two</u> questions — <u>one</u> worth <u>16 marks</u> and the other worth <u>24 marks</u>.

Section A is based on Three Pieces of Non-Fiction Text

1) The <u>five</u> questions in Section A will be based on <u>3 pieces of non-fiction text</u> that you haven't seen before — they'll be in the <u>insert</u> you're given in the exam.

2) You'll need to use <u>one</u> of the texts for <u>each</u> of the first <u>four questions</u> (though two questions will use the same text).

3) Question five will be a <u>comparison</u> question — you'll have to compare two of the three texts, but you get to <u>choose</u> which two texts you compare.

In his exam, James was faced with a type of text he had never seen before.

4) Make sure you read the questions properly so that your answer is about the <u>right text or texts</u>.

Answer All the Questions

1) You have to answer <u>every question</u> in this exam.

2) You should spend about <u>1 hour 15 minutes</u> on Section A and <u>1 hour</u> on Section B. The time you spend on Section A needs to include time to <u>read the texts</u> you've been given.

> It's best to spend about <u>5 minutes reading each text</u> (15 minutes in total), and <u>1 hour writing your answers</u> to Section A — this leaves you with about an hour for Section B.

3) The amount of <u>marks</u> each question is worth affects how much <u>time</u> you should spend on each question — the <u>more marks</u> a question is worth, the <u>more time</u> you should spend on it.

4) In Section A, the first <u>two</u> questions are worth <u>4 marks</u> each — aim to spend about <u>6 minutes</u> on each one. The <u>third</u> question is worth <u>8 marks</u>, so try and spend about <u>12 minutes</u> on it. The <u>fourth</u> and <u>fifth</u> questions are each worth <u>12 marks</u>, so spend about <u>18 minutes</u> on each one.

That's the theory sorted — turn over to see an exam...

Now you know how the exam is structured, I bet you're dying to have a look at an actual paper. Well, I was feeling nice today so I made one just for you — take a look at the next few pages.

Exam Paper — Questions

Here are some lovely <u>example questions</u> to get you in the mood for all that exam fun. The texts for these questions are printed on the next three pages (in the exam they'll be in a separate insert).

Read **Item 1**, the news article called *Adorable Alpacas* and answer the questions below.

1   List 4 things the article tells you about alpacas.

You've got to write down four — or you won't get all the marks.

(4 marks)

2   Why have alpacas become so popular in the UK?

Look for bits in the text that back up this idea.

(4 marks)

Now read **Item 2**, *The British skiing star who's going for gold*, and answer the question below.

3   What reasons can you find in the article for saying that Chemmy Alcott is determined and successful?

Remember to use quotes from the article to back up each of your points.

(8 marks)

Now read **Item 3**, the web page for the charity *Habitat for Humanity*, and answer the question below.

4   How does the writer use language to make the page informative and persuasive to the reader?

(12 marks)

You need to talk about why the page is <u>both</u> informative and persuasive to get the marks.

Now look again at all three items. They have each been presented in a different way.

5   Choose **two** of these items. Compare them using these bullet points:
• the headings and subheadings
• the pictures

This means that you need to write about how the items are <u>similar</u> and how they're <u>different</u>.

(12 marks)

Make some points about each of these bullets — with an example and explanation for each point.

"How did you find the exam?" "It was just on the table..."

All exam questions are fairly similar: compare this, find the reasons for that, list these facts, use these headings to do this, how does this do that... There shouldn't be any big surprises in the exam.

Exam Source — Item 1

Here's Item 1 — the first of the texts for the exam questions on page 42.
It's an article from a news website, and it's all about alpacas.

Adorable Alpacas

These South American animals make great fleecy friends

© iStockphoto.com/Simon Owler

All over England, people are falling in love with a new kind of animal — the alpaca. These adorable creatures are part of the camel family and they come from South America, where they're traditionally kept for their meat and their wool. Now, however, there are around thirty thousand of them in the UK.

You don't need to go to the zoo to see them though — just pop down to your local farm. Farmers all over the UK think they're great — they're well-suited to the weather in the UK, and they can be kept in fields with other animals. Alpacas don't mind long journeys either — you can put them in a trailer or horsebox and they'll just settle down and take a nap! It's not just about their sweet nature though. Their soft and cosy fleeces are in high demand, and farmers have been opening their gates to visitors who'll pay good money just to see them.

Betty Smith, President of Alpaca Lovers UK, says that alpacas make wonderful pets too: "They're quiet, friendly, intelligent, easy to train and gentle with children. You can teach an alpaca to walk on a lead rope and they will happily eat out of your hand. However, if you're going to keep an alpaca, you do need to buy at least two, because alpacas get miserable and stressed when they're alone."

If you think alpacas might be the right kind of pet or farm animal for you, make sure you only buy them from a seller who has been approved by The British Alpaca Society. That way, you can be certain that the alpacas you buy are healthy. The British Alpaca Society also provides help and advice after you've taken your alpacas home.

Alpaca facts:
- Alpacas live for around 20 years.
- Alpaca fleece naturally comes in a range of different colours.
- Alpacas spit when they're angry.
- When they're confused or frightened, alpacas don't attack — they lie down.

Exam Source — Item 2

Here's Item 2 — the second text for those fun-looking exam questions on page 42.
It's an article about the British skier Chemmy Alcott.

The British skiing star who's going for gold

Chemmy Alcott was born on 10th July 1982. She started skiing aged 18 months while on a family trip to France, and skied in her first fun race at the age of three. Now she's a fiercely determined and courageous sportswoman. However, it's taken far more than raw talent for her to become one of the world's top skiers.

Chemmy has been the number one British woman skier since 2003. She is the highest ranked female British skier ever and even challenges the best skiers from more traditional skiing nations. She is also admired by fellow professional skiers for being so determined and dedicated to the sport.

Chemmy in action at the Turin Winter Olympics, 2006

© Sipa Press / Rex Features

Her determination was especially obvious at the Turin Winter Olympics in 2006. For many years, Chemmy had suffered from problems with the bones in her feet, which caused her a lot of pain. Because of this she had missed races and crucial training in the run-up to the Olympic Games. Despite this, she still managed to come 11th in the downhill event. After the 2006 Winter Olympics, Chemmy decided that the only long-term solution for her painful foot problem was surgery. After six months off, Chemmy returned to competitive World Cup skiing in October that year. Skiing pain-free for the first time, she blitzed her way to several top 15 finishes in the downhill, and a career-best of 7th place in the super-combined* after just a couple of days training.

Chemmy started the 2008/09 season with her best ever finish of 10th place in a World Cup Giant Slalom race. Unfortunately the following week Chemmy broke her ankle, but after a quick recovery she finished in 15th place in the Downhill event at the 2009 World Championship, her best result in this event to date.

Chemmy had high hopes for the 2010 Vancouver Winter Olympics. She was fit, healthy and hungry for a medal in one of the five events she was competing in. She managed a series of top 20 finishes and equalled her highest place at the Turin Olympics — 11th in the super-combined event.

*Super-combined skiing — an event made up of two different races, one slalom and one downhill, where the times are added together to give a final result.

Exam Source — Item 3

And finally, here's Item 3. It's a page from the website of the charity Habitat for Humanity.

Accessibility | Site Map | Newsroom | Contact Us

Habitat for Humanity®

Site Search [GO]

Get Involved | Learn About Habitat | Where We Build | Support Habitat | Faces and Places

When the attention of the world has shifted elsewhere we'll still be there picking up the pieces

www.habitatforhumanity.org.uk

Habitat for Humanity

Disaster response
- HFH Resource Centres
- China earthquake
- Myanmar Cyclone
- Bangladesh Cyclone
- Tajikistan earthquake
- Java earthquake
- Tsunami update
- Sign up for news
- Donate

Home >> Learn about Habitat >> Disaster response   - standard font | + larger font   Betsie enhanced   Print

EARTHQUAKE CHINA HELP REBUILD LIVES **Donate Now**

CYCLONE NARGIS MYANMAR **Donate Now**

Disaster Response

After natural disasters and conflicts, Habitat for Humanity is there to pick up the pieces and help renew communities.

When the attention of the world has shifted elsewhere, we'll still be there picking up the pieces

When disaster strikes communities are thrown into trauma and it's vital to get immediate aid to the victims. Whether it's a cyclone, an earthquake or a war, the world's aid agencies are quick to respond.

But what happens when the debris is cleared and the TV cameras have moved on? This is the time that determines if the survivors will live in poverty for years to come or will be able to rebuild their lives. Typically they have now lost everything ... their home, their belongings, their livelihood and even their family and friends. They are now living in makeshift shelters dependent on aid just to survive.

Habitat for Humanity is one of the few international charities entirely dedicated to long-term reconstruction and regeneration. We are committed to helping people rebuild their shattered communities. We are still helping the people of South East Asia in the wake of the Asian Tsunami three and a half years later. Thanks to the overwhelming generosity of our supporters and partners, we have been able to reconstruct more homes in the region than any other Non Government Organisation.

We're there for the long haul

Working through our own organisations on the ground, we work with local people, provide technical expertise and the resources to repair and rebuild homes.

Because we use local materials and simple, practical technology, our work helps to regenerate small local industries. We also provide technical assistance and training to other agencies and their partners, all of which contributes to long-term recovery.

We're guided by clear principles:

- *We see the job through.* We are a specialist long term reconstruction and regeneration agency, providing permanent housing solutions.
- *We build back better.* Future disaster mitigation is a clear priority. Typically, homes are built to better withstand future disasters.
- *We provide local solutions to local problems.* We don't come in with preconceived notions. We start each project with fresh eyes by rigorously assessing the situation, enabling local people to drive the key decisions and responding to the real requirements of the community.

Glossary:
- Regeneration — to make improvements to something so that it's as good as it used to be in the past, or even better.
- Tsunami — a series of giant waves that hit a coastline.
- Non Government Organisation — an organisation that is not controlled by a government, such as a charity.
- Expertise — in-depth knowledge and skills.
- Mitigation — to make something less severe or harmful.
- Preconceived notions — to decide how you're going to do something before you've looked into it.
- Rigorously — to do something thoroughly or in a strict way.

Mark Scheme

These pages will show you just how the examiner would mark the exam on page 42 — so that you know exactly what to do to please them. Ooh, isn't it exciting...

Question 1

> Read **Item 1**, the news article called *Adorable Alpacas* and answer the questions below.
>
> 1   List 4 things the article tells you about alpacas.   *(4 marks)*

This is a pretty simple question. They want you to pick out <u>four things</u> about <u>alpacas</u> from the article.

Number of marks	Possible points	
1 mark for each point made, up to a maximum of 4	alpacas are part of the camel family	alpacas spit when they're angry
	alpacas come from South America	alpacas lie down when confused or frightened
	alpacas are well-suited to UK weather	alpacas are easy to train
	alpacas can be kept with other animals	alpacas are friendly
	alpacas don't mind long journeys	alpacas are gentle with children
	alpacas live for around 20 years	alpacas get stressed when they're alone
	alpaca fleece comes naturally in different colours	

Question 2

> 2   Why have alpacas become so popular in the UK?   *(4 marks)*

The examiners look at a table like the one below and decide which description is the "<u>best fit</u>" for your answer. Then they decide whether you deserve the <u>higher or lower mark</u> for that description.

Number of marks	What you've written	How you've written	How your answer's put together
Band 1 1 mark	One basic point that answers the question.	Confusingly written, copying long sections of text instead of using short quotes.	No obvious structure.
Band 2 2-3 marks	Two or three points that answer the question, with some examples.	Generally clearly written, mostly using short quotes instead of copying long sections of text.	Basic structure, some points are linked together.
Band 3 4 marks	Four clear points that answer the question, with good use of examples.	Clearly and confidently written, using short quotes instead of copying long sections of text.	Clear structure, points are linked together so it's easy to follow.

Mark Scheme

In my day of course they just rolled some dice or prayed to the Greek gods to decide what grade we got. It's a bit more sophisticated now though. Here's how they'd mark <u>question 3</u>.

Question 3

> Now read **Item 2**, *The British skiing star who's going for gold*, and answer the question below.
>
> 3   What reasons can you find in the article for saying that Chemmy Alcott
>   is determined and successful?
>
> *(8 marks)*

In your answer, you could write <u>points like these</u>:

<u>Determined</u>	<u>Successful</u>
• Chemmy "returned to competitive World Cup skiing" six months after having surgery on her foot. • She achieved "several top 15 finishes" after only a few days' training. • She's "admired by fellow professional skiers" for her determination. • She competed in the 2006 Winter Olympics, despite having "missed races and crucial training" because of the pain in her feet. • She competed in the 2009 World Championships despite having recently broken her ankle.	• Since 2003, she's been ranked "the number one British woman skier". • Chemmy is "the highest ranked female British skier ever". • She finished "11th in the downhill event" at the 2006 Winter Olympics. • She came 10th in a World Cup Giant Slalom race. • At the 2010 Winter Olympics she finished "11th in the super-combined event".

Here's how the examiners would mark it:

Number of marks	What you've written	How you've written	How your answer's put together
Band 1 **1-2** **marks**	A couple of basic points made, may only answer one part of the question.	Written in a confusing way, copying long sections of text instead of using short quotes.	No obvious structure.
Band 2 **3-5** **marks**	A few points made that answer both parts of the question, with some examples given.	Generally clearly written, mostly using short quotes instead of copying long sections of text.	Follows a basic structure, with some points linked together.
Band 3 **6-8** **marks**	Several clear points showing the reasons why she is both determined and successful, backed up with good examples.	Clearly and confidently written, using short quotes instead of copying long sections of text.	A well-organised answer with points linked together so it's easy to follow.

Mark Scheme

Question 4

There are <u>12 marks</u> available for this question, so your answer needs to be quite <u>detailed</u>.

> Now read **Item 3**, the web page for the charity *Habitat for Humanity*,
> and answer the question below.
>
> 4   How does the writer use language to make the page informative and persuasive to the reader?
>
> *(12 marks)*

In your answer, you could write <u>points like these</u>:

<u>Informative</u>
• The writer gives clear instructions, such as "Donate Now" to the reader. This makes it clear what the reader needs to do to help the charity.
• The web page includes lots of information about how the charity helps people, for example it says "we use local materials and simple, practical technology". This clearly informs the reader about what will be done with their money if they give a donation.
• The writer uses the rule of three, "a cyclone, an earthquake or a war". This informs the reader about why so many people need help, and also emphasises the range of different problems that the charity faces.

<u>Persuasive</u>
• The writer uses words such as "specialist" and "expertise" to emphasise how much experience the charity has. This shows the reader that their money will be used effectively, so they will be persuaded to make a donation to the charity.
• The web page includes emotive language. Words such as "shattered" and "trauma" make the reader feel sorry for the victims of disasters, so they will be persuaded to make a donation in order to help them.
• The writer uses a rhetorical question, "what happens when the debris is cleared and the TV cameras have moved on?". This makes the reader really think about how little long term help some people receive, which will persuade them to support Habitat for Humanity.

The table below shows what an answer should be like to <u>achieve each mark</u>.

Number of marks	What you've written	How you've written	How your answer's put together
Band 1 1-4 marks	A few basic points about the language used without much explanation about how it makes the page informative and persuasive.	Confusingly written. Often copies from the web page.	Disorganised, with no obvious structure.
Band 2 5-8 marks	Some points that explain how the language used makes the page informative and persuasive.	Generally clearly written, mostly in own words.	Follows a basic structure, with some points linked together.
Band 3 9-12 marks	Several clear points that show how the language used makes the page informative and persuasive, backed up by good examples.	Clearly written in own words with good use of technical terms.	A well-organised answer with points linked together so it's easy to follow.

Mark Scheme

Question 5

> Now look again at all three items. They have each been presented in a different way.
>
> 5   Choose **two** of these items. Compare them using these bullet points:
> - the headings and subheadings
> - the pictures
>   *(12 marks)*

Here are some <u>example points</u>, but remember, you need to make <u>several points</u> like these in your answer to get top marks:

Headings and subheadings	Pictures
The heading of Item 1, "Adorable Alpacas", is informative as it tells the reader that the text is about alpacas. It's also entertaining, as it uses alliteration to emphasise how lovable alpacas are. The heading of Item 3, on the other hand, is purely informative. "Habitat for Humanity" is the name of the charity and it shows that the charity does work to do with homes ("habitat") for people ("humanity"). Alliteration is used here to make the name of the charity more memorable.	Item 1 uses a simple picture to show the reader what alpacas look like. The photo also illustrates the point made in the text that alpacas have "soft and cosy fleeces". The photos in Item 3, however, are more emotive. For example, the photo of the man standing amongst the ruined buildings shows the personal effects disasters can have. This persuades the reader to feel sorry for him, so they will donate money to help him.

Number of marks	What you've written	How you've written	How your answer's put together
Band 1 1-4 marks	A few basic points about the headings or pictures with very little comparison.	Confusingly written, copying sections of both texts.	No clear structure. Points are in a random order.
Band 2 5-8 marks	Some good points about both the headings and the pictures with some comparison of the items.	Fairly well written, mostly in own words.	Answer is organised quite well, with some attempt to link points together.
Band 3 9-12 marks	Several detailed points that compare the headings and pictures used in the items, backed up with good examples.	Thoughtfully and clearly written with confident use of technical terms.	A well-organised answer, with points neatly linked together, so it's easy to follow.

How they work out your Grade

Mark the five questions individually using the mark schemes on pages 46-49.
Then <u>add up</u> the five marks and use the table below to get your mock Unit 1, Section A <u>grade</u>.
(The grade boundaries vary slightly from year to year, but this is a good general guide.)

Of course, your final GCSE grade is an <u>average</u> of this and the <u>rest of your Unit 1 Exam</u>, <u>Unit 2</u> and <u>Unit 3</u>. But the grade you get from this section shows the grade you're <u>on course for</u>.

Marks	8-11	12-15	16-19	20-23	24-40
Grade	G	F	E	D	C

Grade E, D & C Answers to Question 1

This page gives you example answers for question 1, starting with an "E" grade and working up to a "C" grade. Look back at pages 42-45 for the exam questions and texts.

Work out what the article Tells You

1) The question asks for four things the article tells you about alpacas and there are four marks available. That means you get one mark for each fact about alpacas you write down.

2) Scan through the text to see where it tells you about alpacas.

3) Circle the facts about alpacas you find, e.g. "come from South America" and "part of the camel family". Then write down four for your answer.

Here's an example "E" grade answer to the question.

Don't scribble on the book if it belongs to your school — teachers hate that.

1. Alpacas are from South America.
2. Alpacas don't mind long journeys.
3. All over England, people are falling in love with a new kind of animal.
4.

Uh-oh — only three points have been made so the answer can't get four marks.

This doesn't help answer the question so it won't get a mark.

Use your Own Words

1) This is a straightforward question that asks you to make four separate points — the answer even has numbered points to show you what to do.

2) You don't need to use P.E.E. as it only needs a short answer.

This is a "D" grade answer to question 1.

The first three points are good.

1. Alpacas come from South America.
2. They're gentle with children.
3. Alpacas live for around 20 years.
4. Farmers love alpacas.

This point is about farmers, not alpacas, so it wouldn't get a mark.

Make Four clear points

1) Pick out the points you're told in the article and list them in your answer.

2) Make four different points — check that you haven't repeated yourself.

This is a "C" grade answer to question 1.

1. Alpacas are from South America.
2. They're part of the camel family.
3. Alpaca fleece comes in different colours.
4. Alpacas live for around 20 years.

Four clear statements so this answer would get all four marks.

Grade E, D & C Answers to Question 2

That's question 1 out of the way. This page is all about <u>question 2</u>. Let's get ready to party.

Read the article Carefully

1) You need to find the <u>reasons</u> why alpacas have become popular in the UK. Remember, it might not say "alpacas are popular because..." — you'll have to <u>work it out</u> for yourself.

2) This question's worth <u>four marks</u>, so it's a good idea to find <u>four reasons</u> to put in your answer.

Here's an <u>"E" grade</u> answer to question 2.

> These facts are right, but they don't answer the question.

> Alpacas come from South America. They are in the camel family. People like them because they're traditionally kept for their meat and their wool. People like to keep them as pets because they're friendly and quiet.

> This explains why alpacas have become popular.

> This bit's copied from the text — it should be in quotation marks to show it's a quote.

This answer only gives <u>one reason</u> why alpacas have become popular, so it wouldn't get many marks.

Use Quotes to Back Up your points

1) Try and work <u>short quotes</u> into your answer to <u>support</u> your points.

2) Make sure all your points <u>answer the question</u> — don't make a point if it's not about why alpacas have become popular in the UK.

This is a <u>"D" grade</u> answer to question 2.

> The article doesn't say this is why they're popular in the UK so it wouldn't get a mark.

> Alpacas are really popular in England. People like them because they have a "sweet nature". Farmers like them because they have got wool that they can sell. They can keep them for their meat as well.

> Good use of a short quotation.

This answer makes a couple of <u>good points</u>, but not enough to get full marks.

Stick to the Question

1) Your answer doesn't need to be very <u>long</u>. There are only four marks available, so you should try to make <u>four clear points</u>.

2) Use <u>quotation marks</u> when quoting bits of the article, and try to keep your quotes <u>short</u> and <u>to the point</u>.

This is a <u>"C" grade</u> answer to question 2.

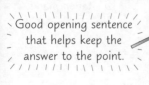
> Good opening sentence that helps keep the answer to the point.

> Alpacas have become popular in the UK because they have a "sweet nature" and are "easy to train", which makes them ideal as pets. Farmers like them because they are easy to keep with other animals, and they can get money for alpaca fleeces. They're also "well-suited" to the British weather and people will pay to come and look at them.

> Quote built into text — examiners love this.

Grade E & D Answers to Question 3

Question 3 is worth <u>8 marks</u> so it needs a <u>longer answer</u>. Take another look at the exam on pages 42-45, then dive right into these <u>"E"</u> and <u>"D" grade answers</u>. The "C" grade answer is on the next page.

You need to write about both Chemmy's Success and Determination

1) This question is worth <u>8 marks</u>, so try and make <u>8 points</u> — <u>four</u> reasons why Chemmy Alcott is <u>determined</u> and <u>four</u> reasons why she's <u>successful</u>.

2) The space for your answer is <u>divided up</u> into two sections to help you <u>organise</u> your writing.

Here's an <u>"E" grade</u> answer to the question.

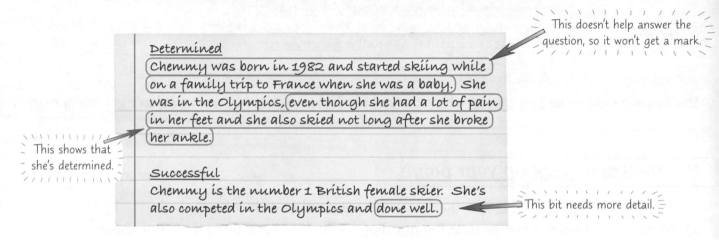

This doesn't help answer the question, so it won't get a mark.

Determined
Chemmy was born in 1982 and started skiing while on a family trip to France when she was a baby. She was in the Olympics, even though she had a lot of pain in her feet and she also skied not long after she broke her ankle.

This shows that she's determined.

Successful
Chemmy is the number 1 British female skier. She's also competed in the Olympics and done well.

This bit needs more detail.

Work Short Quotes into your answer

1) Use <u>quotes</u> to support your points — try and work <u>short ones</u> into your answer wherever you can.

2) <u>Organise</u> your answer — be careful that you don't talk about her success in the determination section and vice versa.

Here's a <u>"D" grade</u> answer to question 3.

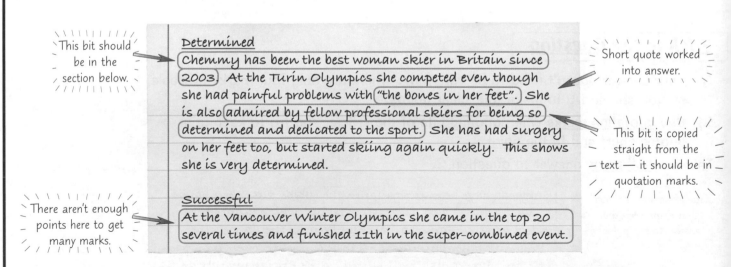

This bit should be in the section below.

Short quote worked into answer.

Determined
Chemmy has been the best woman skier in Britain since 2003. At the Turin Olympics she competed even though she had painful problems with "the bones in her feet". She is also admired by fellow professional skiers for being so determined and dedicated to the sport. She has had surgery on her feet too, but started skiing again quickly. This shows she is very determined.

This bit is copied straight from the text — it should be in quotation marks.

There aren't enough points here to get many marks.

Successful
At the Vancouver Winter Olympics she came in the top 20 several times and finished 11th in the super-combined event.

This answer is pretty good — but the second part needs <u>more detail</u> to get more marks.

Grade C Answer to Question 3

There's an example "C" grade answer for <u>question 3</u> on this page. It's more thrilling than cycling blindfolded down the side of a mountain in the middle of winter whilst wearing a silly hat. And I can tell you from experience, that's pretty thrilling.

Write the Same Amount for Each Part of the question

1) Go back to the text and <u>circle</u> the bits about Chemmy's <u>determination</u>, e.g. "admired by fellow professional skiers for being so determined".

2) Then <u>underline</u> the things the text tells you about Chemmy's <u>success</u>, e.g. "number one British woman skier since 2003".

3) Hey presto, you can use the bits you've circled and underlined as a <u>plan</u> for your answer.

4) This is one of the nice, straightforward "<u>search and find</u>" questions. Have a look at the advice on <u>page 38</u> and it should be a walk in the park.

Here's a "<u>C</u>" grade answer to question 3.

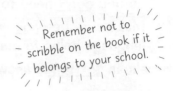
Remember not to scribble on the book if it belongs to your school.

Pippa was determined to look good on the ski slopes.

This sentence tells the examiner that these points are going to be about her determination.

Determined
We learn that Chemmy is determined because she competes with the best skiers from other countries, despite not being from one of the "traditional skiing nations". She's also admired by other professional skiers for being "determined and dedicated". She even skied in the Turin Olympics, after only a few days' training and in a lot of pain from her feet. She also competed in the 2009 World Championship despite having recently broken an ankle.

Good use of quotation.

Provides evidence to show that she's determined.

Successful
One of the reasons for saying that Chemmy is successful is that she has been the best "British woman skier since 2003". She is also "the highest ranked female British skier ever". In the 2006 Turin Winter Olympics she came 11th in the downhill event and in the 2010 Olympics, "11th in the super-combined event". However, she's finished even higher than this at other competitions — her best ever result in the super-combined event is 7th place in a World Cup competition.

Lots of precise detail from the text — just what the examiner wants to see.

This answer makes several clear points that answer <u>both</u> parts of the question. There are also lots of good <u>examples</u> and some <u>short quotes</u> worked into the text.

Grade E & D Answers to Question 4

On to question 4 now. Here's an "E" grade and a "D" grade answer for you to enjoy.

You need to focus on Language

1) This question is asking about how the writer has used language — so you don't need to talk about how the page has been presented.

2) Make sure you link each point back to the question — you need to say how the language helps to make the page either informative or persuasive.

Here's an "E" grade answer to the question.

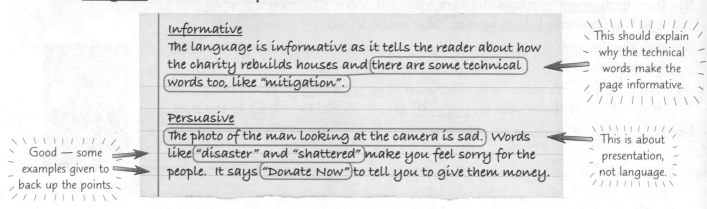

Informative
The language is informative as it tells the reader about how the charity rebuilds houses and there are some technical words too, like "mitigation".

Persuasive
The photo of the man looking at the camera is sad. Words like "disaster" and "shattered" make you feel sorry for the people. It says "Donate Now" to tell you to give them money.

This should explain why the technical words make the page informative.

This is about presentation, not language.

Good — some examples given to back up the points.

This answer needs to give more explanation about how the language used makes the page informative and persuasive.

Think about the Effect of the Language

1) Go through the text and put a letter I next to the language features that are informative.

2) Put a letter P next to the language features that are persuasive.

3) This will give you a basic plan so you'll be ready to start writing.

This is a "D" grade answer to the question.

This is about how the web page is informative, but it's got nothing to do with language.

Informative
I think the web page is informative because I learnt a lot from it. It uses informative language when it describes how people have lost "their home, their belongings, their livelihood and even their family and friends", so you know that people are affected badly. The words "Donate Now" are written twice to make the page informative because the reader is told what they should do next.

Persuasive
Saying "When the attention of the world has shifted elsewhere we'll still be there picking up the pieces" makes you think that Habitat for Humanity are the only charity that will keep helping people when everyone else has gone home. This will persuade you to give money because it sounds like the charity really needs help. Words like "trauma" and "shattered communities" make you feel sorry for the people in the disasters too.

This is good — it explains how the language used makes the page persuasive.

This just needs to link the effect on the reader to what they're being persuaded to do.

Grade C Answer to Question 4

Here's a lovely "C" grade answer to <u>question 4</u>. Aren't I nice. Well, to be honest, it would be nicer if I made you a delicious chocolate cake to take your mind off revision, but unfortunately my oven blew up last week, and cooking things on the radiator isn't very successful.

Use lots of Examples to Back Up your points

1) This question's worth <u>12 marks</u>, so it needs a longer answer.
2) Try and write about the <u>same amount</u> for how language is used to make the page <u>informative</u>, and how it's used to make it <u>persuasive</u>.
3) For every <u>language feature</u> you mention, make sure you say what <u>effect</u> it has.
4) For questions like this, the <u>quality</u> of your writing is also important — so try to write <u>clearly</u> and check your <u>spelling</u> and <u>punctuation</u>.

Here's a <u>"C" grade</u> answer to question 4.

Ernie's language wasn't informative <u>or</u> persuasive — but then, he was a horse.

Good opening statement — it links the answer back to the question straight away.

This explains how the language makes the page informative.

It's good to use the odd technical term, as long as you're sure you know what it means.

Use lots of short quotes to back up your points.

Informative

The web page informs the reader about the charity's work. The first sentence says that Habitat for Humanity works in areas affected by "natural disasters and conflicts" and it helps to "pick up the pieces and help renew communities". The language is simple, so it's really clear what the charity does. It says "We are still helping the people of South East Asia" to inform the reader about the good things the charity has actually done, so it makes the reader trust the charity more. The web page uses a rule of three when it says "a cyclone, an earthquake or a war". This is to show the different types of disaster that can affect people and it also shows the range of problems that the charity is faced with.

Persuasive

Emotive language such as "trauma", "disaster" and "shattered" makes the reader feel sorry for the people affected by the disasters. This persuades the reader to donate money to try to help them. Saying "what happens when the debris is cleared and the TV cameras have moved on?" is a rhetorical question. It makes the reader think for themselves and realise that the victims don't get much long term help. This will persuade them to support Habitat for Humanity as they are "one of the few" charities that provide this kind of help. The web page also uses reassuring language, such as "we see the job through" and "we build back better" to write about how the charity works. This persuades the reader to support the charity as it makes them feel that Habitat for Humanity do a good job.

This is a really good answer — it makes some <u>thoughtful points</u>, backed up with <u>examples</u> from the text and clearly <u>answers the question</u>.

Grade E & D Answers to Question 5

Question 5's a bit more tricky because you have to <u>compare</u> two texts. Here's a sample "E" and a sample "D" grade answer. Head back to pages 42-45 to remind yourself about the exam questions.

You have to Compare two texts

1) This question's all about <u>comparing</u> — that means you need to write about the <u>similarities</u> and <u>differences</u> between two texts.

2) You get to <u>choose</u> which two texts you compare for this question.

3) Your answer needs to cover <u>both</u> of the <u>bullet points</u> in the question (in this case, that's 'headings and subheadings' and 'pictures').

Here's an <u>"E" grade</u> answer to question 5.

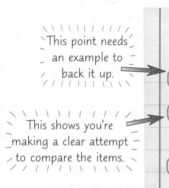
This point needs an example to back it up.

This shows you're making a clear attempt to compare the items.

There's no comparison of the two items in this paragraph.

This point needs to fully explain the effect of this photo on the reader.

> Item 3 has lots of different headings and subheadings. The heading is quite easy to remember and then there are some other subheadings too. Item 1 has a heading about alpacas and that shows that the article is going to be about alpacas. The pictures in the articles are there for different reasons. The photo in Item 1 shows an alpaca and you can see that it looks soft and fluffy. Item 3 shows some photos of people who need help like the picture of the man standing next to his house that has been ruined.

Focus on the Headings, Subheadings and Pictures

1) Make sure you <u>back up</u> any points you make with <u>examples</u> or <u>quotes</u> from the text.

2) Stick to the point — this question's only asking about <u>headings</u>, <u>subheadings</u> and <u>pictures</u>, so you should only write about those things.

This is a <u>"D" grade</u> answer to the question.

Remember to say what the effect on the reader is.

Don't just count the subheadings — say what effect they have and compare them to the other item.

This shows that you're making a comparison.

> The heading in Item 1, "Adorable Alpacas", tells the reader that the article is about alpacas. The heading is short to quickly show the information, and it is in bold so it is more eye-catching. The heading of Item 3, "Habitat for Humanity" is also in bold, and it shows the reader what the text will be about. Item 1 has a subheading at the top and one at the bottom, but Item 3 has lots more subheadings.
> The picture in Item 1 shows the reader what an alpaca looks like. It also backs up the text that says that alpacas are "fleecy" and people will think that alpacas are "adorable" when they see the picture. The pictures in Item 3 are informative too as they show the problems disaster victims have. For example, there is a picture of a man standing next to a ruined building. He looks sad, so the pictures in Item 3 are supposed to make the reader feel sorry for the disaster victims as well.

Grade C Answer to Question 5

Woo-hoo, last page in this section. Actually, it's the last page in the book, except for a nifty little <u>glossary</u> and <u>index</u> that I've put together for you. So just have a look at this <u>"C" grade answer</u>, then you can reward yourself with a nice cup of tea.

Write a Detailed answer in your Own Words with Supporting Quotes

1) There are <u>12 marks</u> available for this question, so make sure you put <u>plenty of detail</u> into your answer.

2) For this question, there won't be any <u>headings</u> on the answer paper to write under, so you'll need to think of a way to <u>structure</u> the answer yourself. There are loads of ways you could do this, for example, you could try putting each comparison you make in its <u>own paragraph</u>.

This is a <u>"C" grade</u> answer to question 5.

"Adorable Alpacas" uses alliteration to make it sound quite light-hearted, so you can tell from the heading that the article is for a younger audience. The heading of Item 3, "Habitat for Humanity", also uses alliteration. However, in Item 3 the alliteration is used to emphasise the name of the charity, so people will remember it.

> This is really good — it's explained the different effects of using alliteration in both titles.

The subheading near the top of Item 1, "These South American animals make great fleecy friends" is similar to the title as it tells the reader some information. The subheadings in Item 3 are different because they persuade you to support the charity. For example, the subheading "We're there for the long haul" is persuasive because it shows that the charity is responsible because it supports people in the long term.

> This needs much more explanation.

The photo in Item 1 is used to inform and entertain. It shows the reader what an alpaca looks like and it also shows that alpacas are "Adorable" as some people might think the alpaca looks nice in the photograph. The photos in Item 3 are used to persuade, so it is different from Item 1. For example, there is a photo of a man standing in some ruins. He's looking right at the reader, so they would be persuaded to donate money to help him.

> This makes it really clear that a comparison is being made.

The photo of the alpaca in Item 1 backs up a lot of the things the text says about alpacas. For example, the alpaca looks very "fleecy" and it also looks "quiet" and "gentle". In Item 3 the photo of the man pulling the cart along is blurred and he looks like he is in a hurry to help someone. This makes you think the charity's work is really urgent.

> Always make sure you give an example whenever you make a point.

This is a really good answer — it has a <u>clear structure</u> and makes a lot of <u>thoughtful points</u>, backed up with <u>examples</u> from the texts.

Sean the sheep knew his days as England's number one fleecy friend were numbered.

Glossary

alliteration	Where words in a phrase have the same sound repeated. It's often used to make a phrase stand out. E.g. "the bold, brash beat of the band".
audience	The people who an author wants to read their writing.
bias	Giving more support to one point of view than to another, due to the writer's own opinions affecting the way they write.
broadsheet	A newspaper which is considered to be more serious and respectable than tabloid newspapers. E.g. The Daily Telegraph or The Guardian.
caption	A line of text under a photograph or picture, telling you what it shows.
contrast	When two things are described in a way which emphasises how different they are. E.g. a writer might contrast two different places, or two different attitudes.
empathy	When someone feels like they understand what someone else is experiencing and how they feel about it.
emotive language	Language that appeals to your emotions, to try and get you to feel something e.g. anger or happiness.
exaggeration	Describing something as more than it really is. E.g. "A million miles from home".
first person	A personal style of writing, using words like "I", "me", "mine", "we", "us", "our" etc.
font	The style and size of lettering used.
headline	The statement at the top of a text (e.g. a newspaper article), usually in a large font, used to attract readers' interest by giving an impression of what the text is about.
imagery	Language that creates a picture in your mind, bringing the text to life.
implication	When a writer gives an impression that something is the case without saying it outright. E.g. "Last time I left Humphrey in charge, the house nearly burnt down" — this implies that Humphrey can't be trusted, without saying it directly.
irony	Saying one thing but meaning the opposite. E.g. "What a great idea of mine to go for a nice long walk on the rainiest day of the year."
language	The choice of words used. The language controls the effect the piece of writing will have on the reader, e.g. it can be emotive or persuasive.
layout	The way a piece of writing is visually presented to the reader. E.g. what kind of font is used, whether there are subheadings, the use of photographs, whether text columns are used, and anything else that affects the way a text looks.
media	Any way of communicating with large numbers of people, e.g. newspapers, TV, radio, films, websites, magazines.
metaphor	A way of describing something by saying that it is something else, to create a strong image. E.g. "His eyes were deep, black, oily pools."
non-fiction	Writing which is about the real world, rather than a made up story.

Glossary

onomatopoeia	A word that <u>sounds like</u> what it's supposed to mean. E.g. "buzz", "crunch", "bang", "pop", "ding".
personification	A special kind of description where you write about something as if it's a <u>person</u> or animal with thoughts or feelings. E.g. "The sea growled hungrily."
pun	A "play on words" — a word or phrase that's deliberately used because it has <u>more than one meaning</u>. E.g. "She lies on the couch at the psychiatrist's", where "lies" could mean "lies down" or "tells lies".
purpose	The <u>reason</u> someone writes a text. E.g. to persuade, to argue, to advise.
rhetoric	<u>Language</u> techniques that are designed to achieve a specific <u>effect</u>, e.g. repetition or exaggeration to make a speech more persuasive.
rhetorical question	A question which <u>doesn't need an answer</u>. E.g. "Are we really expected to put up with this government's lies?"
sarcasm	Saying something in a cutting, <u>nasty</u> way, often using <u>irony</u>. E.g. "Well done mate, another failed exam, you really are a bright spark."
simile	A way of describing something by <u>comparing</u> it to something else, usually by using the words "like" or "as". E.g. "He was as pale as the moon," or "Her hair was like a bird's nest."
slang	Words or phrases that sound <u>informal</u> or <u>conversational</u>, e.g. "bloke", "telly", "stop going on about it".
stereotype	An inaccurate, <u>generalised</u> view of a particular <u>group of people</u>. E.g. a stereotype of football fans might be that they're all hooligans.
strapline	A short statement <u>under the headline</u> that gives <u>more information</u> about what the following article is about. The text is smaller than the main headline.
structure	The <u>order</u> and <u>arrangement</u> of a piece of writing. E.g. how the text begins, develops and ends, whether it uses subheadings or not, etc.
style	The <u>way</u> a text is <u>written</u>, e.g. the type of language and techniques used.
subheading	A word or phrase that <u>stands out</u> from the text and <u>divides</u> the text into chunks. It gives an idea of what the <u>next section</u> of text is about.
tabloid	A newspaper with <u>short</u>, almost square pages, e.g. The Sun or The Mirror, often thought of as less serious than broadsheets.
text	Any piece of <u>writing</u>, e.g. an article, a speech, a leaflet.
text formatting	Ways of making bits of text <u>stand out</u>, e.g. **bold**, *italic*, <u>underlining</u>, CAPITALS.
tone	The <u>mood</u> of a piece of writing, e.g. happy, sad, serious, lighthearted. It's an overall effect, created by things like choice of words, imagery and layout.
vocabulary	The range of <u>words</u> used by a writer or in a specific text.

Index